GUIDANCE MONOGRAPH SERIES

Shelley C. Stone

Bruce Shertzer

Editors

GUIDANCE MONOGRAPH SERIES

The general purpose of Houghton Mifflin's Guidance Monograph Series is to provide high quality coverage of topics which are of abiding importance in contemporary counseling and guidance practice. In a rapidly expanding field of endeavor, change and innovation are inevitably present. A trend accompanying such growth is greater and greater specialization. Specialization results in an increased demand for materials which reflect current modifications in guidance practice while simultaneously treating the field in greater depth and detail than commonly found in textbooks and brief journal articles.

The list of eminent contributors to this series assures the reader expert treatment of the areas covered. The monographs are designed for consumers with varying familiarity to the counseling and guidance field. The editors believe that the series will be useful to experienced practitioners as well as beginning students. While these groups may use the monographs with somewhat different goals in mind, both will benefit from the treatment given to content areas.

The content areas treated have been selected because of specific criteria. Among them are timeliness, practicality, and persistency of the issues involved. Above all, the editors have attempted to select topics which are of major substantive concern to counseling and guidance personnel.

Shelley C. Stone

Bruce Shertzer

INTEGRATIVE
COUNSELING AND
PSYCHOTHERAPY

DARRELL SMITH

STATE UNIVERSITY OF NEW YORK
COLLEGE AT ONEONTA

HOUGHTON MIFFLIN COMPANY · BOSTON

ATLANTA · DALLAS · GENEVA, ILL. · HOPEWELL, N.J. · PALO ALTO

ISBN: 0–395–200334

Library of Congress Catalog Card
Number: 74–11957

DEDICATION

....

To my wife, Joanne, and children, Ruth, Chris, and Caroline,
whose love, friendship, and companionship
have been integrative forces in my life.

CONTENTS

LIST OF FIGURES

EDITORS' INTRODUCTION

This monograph brings together an extensive amount of material from diverse sources on counseling and psychotherapy in an effort to present an integrative position. In a lucid and literate style, Darrell Smith cogently and persuasively sets forth a reasoned argument for utilizing many techniques from many sources selectively. At no time does he suggest or encourage theoretical dilettantism. Indeed, he clearly discourages the all too prevalent view of the eclectic counselor as a butterfly flitting from one theoretical approach to another, collecting a little of the nectar of techniques here and a little there, and perhaps picking up an occasional dusting of conceptual pollen only to scrape it off at the next stop. Smith's material is based on a soundly reasoned argument urging the counselor-therapist to strive to integrate concepts and techniques from as many sources as possible and to utilize this procedure for the benefit of the client.

Dr. Smith's monograph expresses his own personalized view of counseling and psychotherapy and in that sense he allows much of himself to show through. His presentation is scholarly, highly informative, very readable and yet realistic and practical. We commend it to professional counselors and students in the field.

SHELLEY C. STONE
BRUCE SHERTZER

AUTHOR'S INTRODUCTION

Numerous systems of counseling and psychotherapy have emerged since the formulation of Freudian psychoanalysis at the turn of this century. Each new system has purported, on one ground or another, to be the "best" psychotherapeutic approach to the comprehension and modification of human behavior. This volume claims that no single theory encompasses *the* truth about the nature of man and behavior change; rather, a truly comprehensive theory of counseling and psychotherapy lies in the integration of the best elements derived from the multiplicity of existing systems.

The basic purpose of this work is to demonstrate how an integrative counseling and psychotherapy may be developed in a systematic, scientific, and consistent manner. The content included represents the author's personal view of counseling and therapy. Having no intentions whatsoever to be prescriptive, I desire that this volume might serve as a model to those colleagues who wish to follow an integrative path.

The reader will observe considerable use of masculine pronouns throughout this monograph. This choice was made for the sake of writing convenience and apart from any desire to play sexual politics. Therefore, except where the gender is clearly defined, the "masculine" terms refer generically to human beings.

D. S.

1

Preliminary Observations

A Psychological Redress*

Three score and some years ago a man of great genius brought forth a new psychological system conceived in the treatment of hysteria and neuroses and founded on the assumption that all behavior is biologically and psychically determined.

Since then numerous psychotherapies have emerged and engaged themselves in a "civil war" contesting whether that system or any system established on such limited and deterministic premises can adequately account for human development and behavior change. We are now met on the "battlefield" of that feud between conflicting systems of psychotherapy. We have come as integrationists to explore the many approaches to the field of counseling and psychotherapy and to provide a "resting place" for the diverse principles and concepts of those theorists who have invested their lives in order that psychotherapy might be well-established and advanced as a profession. It is altogether fitting and proper that we should do this integrative study.

We humbly acknowledge that we cannot create, we cannot for-

* Apologies to Abraham Lincoln.

1

mulate, we cannot initiate a fresh and unique approach to psychotherapy. The creative and pioneering individuals, living and dead, who struggled in the development and evolution of this profession have been productive far above our meager power to add or detract. The world of psychotherapy will little note nor long remember what we say here, but it can never forget what our predecessors have contributed to this still emerging profession. It is for us to be dedicated to the unfinished work which they have thus far advanced. It is for us to be devoted to the great task of integrating the diverse psychotherapies rather than perpetuating the conflict between them. It is time to bury the polemic hatchet and to begin to build unitedly and with appreciation upon the foundations already laid. Let us finally resolve that no one theorist or theory presents the *total* psychotherapy knowledge nor is any theory void of *any* valid knowledge but that each theorist or theory represents *certain aspects* of the total body of knowledge. Let us work integratively to give the profession a new sense of vitality, openness, cooperativeness, and unity. Let us collaborate to build a psychotherapy profoundly concerned with the advancement and amelioration of the welfare of mankind (rather than founding, promoting, and defending proprietary schools of psychological thought); a psychotherapy designed to accommodate the developmental and adjustmental concerns of all people (rather than limited approaches geared for select and/or elitist clienteles); a psychotherapy which need not perish from but flourish on the earth.

Emergence of Divergent Theories

Contemporary psychotherapy owes its existence in a large measure to the pioneering work of Sigmund Freud. Since hypnosis was the precursor of psychoanalysis, perhaps we should add that psychotherapy today is remotely indebted to Jean Charcot and Josef Breuer, two skilled hypnotherapists who were mentors to Freud. Freud and Breuer collaborated in their Vienna practices from about 1885 to around 1900. They coauthored the landmark work *Studies of Hysteria* in 1893. About that time Freud and Breuer began to part company due to conflicting theories of the etiology of hysteria and neurosis. At the turn of the century Freud launched his own system.

The publication of [his] two great initial works, *The Interpretation of Dreams* ... and *The Psychopathology of Everyday Life* ... in the

1900–1901 period . . . marked Freud's beginning as the father of psychoanalysis and, indeed, as the father of modern personality theory. [Rychlak, 1973, p. 28]

In a short time a number of disciples were attracted to the founder of the new movement. Among the original followers of Freud and psychoanalysis were Alfred Adler, Carl Jung, Otto Rank, Karl Abraham, Sandor Ferenczi, Wilhelm Reich, William Stekel, Paul Federn, and Ernest Jones. Freud was unable to hold the friendship and loyalty of most of these equally ambitious men. Surprisingly soon Freud's disciples established their own schools of thought in outspoken rebellion against the master (Munroe, 1955).

Adler was the first devotee to separate himself bitterly and permanently from Freud. Several factors precipitated the severance of the relationship, but the major issue appears to have been the marked difference in viewpoints regarding the underlying cause of neurosis. Adler sought to find the answer in man's struggle for power or superiority in order to overcome the feeling of inferiority in contrast to Freud's theory of sexual dynamics (Thompson, 1950). The break with Freud was final in 1911, and Adler was on his way to establish a new psychological school.

The next student to abandon the Freudian camp was Jung. Jung, too, differed with Freud on the sexual etiology of neurosis, and Freud was infuriated when his disciple had the audacity to redefine libido as a general life energy which could not be reduced to more sexual terms. The controversy over the nature of the libido along with Freud's dissatisfaction with Jung's interest in mysticism and future-oriented therapy led to a separation in 1913. Jung proceeded to develop his own approach to therapy.

A similiar pattern followed with Rank and the other members of the primal psychoanalytic coterie.

Since the severing feuds between Freud and his hand-picked successor and crown-prince, Carl Jung, and his band of short-lived understudies, there has been a proliferation of theoretical approaches to psychotherapy. The following is a representative sample of the systems of psychotherapy which have emerged to counteract Freudian psychoanalysis *and* one another: Individual Psychology (Adler), Analytical Psychology (Jung), Will Therapy (Rank), Relaxation Therapy (Ferenczi), Active Analytic Psychotherapy (Stekel), Orgone Therapy (Reich), Character Analysis (Horney), Psychobiologic Therapy (Meyer), Interpersonal Psychotherapy (Sullivan), Dynamic Psychotherapy (Alexander), Social-Psychological Analysis (Fromm), Existential Analysis or *Daseinanalyse* (Binswanger and Boss), Logotherapy (Frankl), Conditioned Reflex Therapy (Salter), Fixed Role Therapy (Kelly), Gestalt Therapy (Perls), Client-Centered Therapy (Rogers), Rational-Emotive Psychotherapy (Ellis), Behavior Therapy (Bandura, Lazarus, and Wolpe), Reality Therapy (Glasser), Transactional Analysis (Berne), Encounter (Schutz), and Provocative Therapy (Farrelly & Brandsma). To illustrate that this listing is a mere sampling of psychotherapies, Harper (1959) has identified and elaborated on what he considered to be the 36 main systems of psychological treatment *which relied primarily on verbal exchanges* between therapist and client; Jurjevich (1973) places "28 American originals" under the rubric of *direct psychotherapy;* and Cunningham and Peters (1973) have entered 43 different approaches in their compilation of *individual* counseling theories. An exhaustive registration of historical and current psychotherapies would probably include hundreds of entries.

Each "new" system of therapy faults, to some degree, its predecessors and claims a superior status to them in terms of either a) the conceptualizations of the nature of man and human behavior, or b) the desired goal(s) for the therapy process, or c) the appropriate procedures and methods to be used, or d) some combination of these factors. A survey of the theories of counseling and psychotherapy leads an investigator to surmise that a great many of the "original" theorists were somewhat blind to the ideas of others. There is ample support for the maxim stated first by the Hebrew sage and applied later by Boring (1929) that "there is nothing new under the sun."

> I have tried to show for psychology . . . that nothing which is supposed to be new is ever really new. . . . Careful scrutiny of a creative imagination seems to reveal little that is brand-new. The ideas occur as the result of individual thinking, or the facts are found as the result of experiment, both are put forward, and nothing much happens. Then, perhaps many years later, someone comes along, sees relationships, puts things together and formulates a great theory or founds a great movement. . . . Often the formulator or founder is not even the compounder, but another man, who because of his personality or because of the times in which he speaks, has the capacity for gaining attention. So he originates . . . a new step in progress, lending his name to a theory or a school. [Boring, p. 114]

Denominational Psychotherapy

A striking similarity can be detected between the parochialism which characterizes a good many of the therapy systems and religious denominationalism.

> . . . each school was founded by a charismatic leader who attracted loyal disciples. They, with their students, worked in partisan-like

fashion to demonstrate the value and validity of their orientation . . . Freudians, Jungians, Adlerians, Sullivanians, Rogerians . . . each group having little, if any, communication with the others. At times, one gets the impression that there is much duplication of effort and wasted energy in these groups as they go about rediscovering each other's principles and as they go about coining new terms for theories and techniques that are practically synonymous with or special cases of already existing ones. [Stein, 1961, pp. 5–6]

Di Loreto (1971) labels the era prior to the experimental investigation of psychotherapy as "academic tribalism." He asserts that

The various schools of psychotherapy which existed consisted of more or less loosely organized theoretical formulations based on biased and unsystematic observations. . . . Consequently, adherence to any of these theoretical views was based on faith, conviction, and personal satisfaction; and loyalties were maintained and perpetuated by identification with a particular set of esoteric rituals. . . . With little more than faith and the sheer force of opinion to back their untested propositions and doctrinaire assertions, it is not surprising that these so-called coteries or "schools" existed as factious, often diametrically opposed to one another in terms of their aims, methods, and goals. . . . Most [currently] existing schools of psychotherapy are based as much, if not more, on faith and dogma as on comparatively derived research findings. By worshipping their flimsy hypotheses into truth and then selecting "research" to bolster their already well developed personal convictions, these schools become implacable and categorically indestructible . . . immune to dissonant empirical findings. [pp. 2, 7]

Wolberg (1954) has observed that the parochial bias in psychotherapy

usually takes the form of a flaunting of one's special brand of therapy as superior or "best." This is confounding when one considers that the practice of psychotherapy [supposedly] is rooted in empiricism. Nevertheless, there are those who, wedded to a specific school of psychotherapeutic thinking, espouse their theories with as great vehemence as they denounce and depreciate those of other schools. [p. 106]

Ford and Urban (1963) throw additional light on the religiosity which is prevalent among psychotherapies.

This multiplicity of theory and techniques, untested and sometimes untestable by systematic, controlled, and repeatable procedures, has led some zealots to give the status of fact to what originally were offered frankly as hypotheses. They have tended to convert into dogma what was originally offered as theory to be tested and revised. Polemics . . . sometimes have been the avenues chosen to settle theoretical disputes. Enthusiastic proponents of various points of view sometimes have seemed to imply that one set of procedures is appropriate for all problems and to ignore the possibility that their set of procedures may be severely limited in applicability. [p. 15]

Thorne (1961, 1967, 1973a) has been brash enough to ascribe the term "cultist" to those individuals who affiliate themselves with a single school. In his judgment, the criteria of cultism include

general failure to relate new developments historically and acknowledge theoretical antecedents, coining esoteric new vocabularies operationally unrelated to basic science factors, establishing proprietary schools and groups dedicated to the advancement of the method, failure to conduct proper standardization and outcome studies, preoccupation with cultistic methods to the exclusion of established clinical knowledge, uncritical enthusiasm and claims for own methods, improper advertising, and unsuitable ego involvement on the part of advocates. [Thorne, 1973a, p. 849]

No doubt there were many good and many bad motives and reasons involved in the creation of the situation described above. We might guess that a number of theories have been promoted by eager aspirants who wished to achieve recognition and find their place in the sun. Perhaps we should expect each profession to have its share of *prima donnas*. But surely some of the psychotherapies were developed out of unpretentious and altruistic motivation. Maskin (1960) and Stein (1961) have suggested that a plausible reason for the proliferation of diverse psychotherapies is the difference in types of clients on which the founders of the different schools based their initial observations.

We could search farther for the causative forces of the divergence in psychotherapeutic thinking and give detailed expositions of these differences, but this would be of minuscule benefit to our cause. A more worthy objective to work toward is that of synthesizing and systematizing the elements of the apparently contradictory psychotherapies to form a larger superordinate system.

Spirit of Integration

The very existence of many feuding and contradicting theories and methods of psychotherapy suggests that the whole body of psychotherapeutic truth* is not to be found in a single system. If our observation is valid, then the following should hold: 1) each of

* Truth in this context has reference to the conformity with and/or the reproducibility in reality of the concepts, principles, procedures, and methods employed to define man and the human situation and to effect the desired change(s) in behavior.

the theories represents certain unique aspects of the total truth; 2) all bona fide systems of therapy share admittedly some basic elements of the truth; 3) most of the theories hold in common many components of the truth but either fail to recognize them or refuse to admit them openly due to the egotistical preoccupation of each theorist with his own system; and 4) the whole psychotherapeutic truth can be realized *only* through a systematic and progressive integration of the truth-parts found in the many diverse psychotherapies.

A growing number of psychologists and psychotherapists have advocated the integrative approach to the understanding and improvement of the human situation. This section has as its aim to trace nonexhaustively the history of integrative psychology and psychotherapy.

Selected General Emphases

William James, the psychologist turned philosopher, sought to reconcile the "tender-minded" rationalists and the "tough-minded" empiricists via the *pragmatic method.* James' open-mindedness, pluralistic stance, and dedication to the search for truth through multiple avenues are admirably demonstrated in his *Pragmatism* (1907). Pragmatism, in the mind of James, is a mediator and reconciler which eschews fixed principles, dogma, pretense of finality in truth, and closed systems. It is concerned with openness, facts and concreteness, consequences, experimentation, and action. The pragmatic method, characterized by a flexible empiricist attitude, invites the application of any and all principles, concepts, ideas, and methods which can be assimilated, validated, corroborated and verified in reality.

The epithet "middle-of-the-roader" was chosen and self-ascribed by Robert Woodworth (1931, 1948, 1964) to identify his position. Woodworth recognized that schools of psychology begin as a revolt against the established order and tend sometimes to be excessive. He was fearful that psychology would be viewed externally as a profession divided against itself; and, for a half-century, he encouraged the rapprochement of warring factions. He saw some good in every psychological school but none of them were ideal. Woodworth maintained that each school or system has its special line of work and makes its contribution to the whole of psychological knowledge, but no single one possesses the final answer.

Van Kaam (1963, 1966) proposes that the existential outlook provides both the attitude and the foundation for a comprehensive theory of man and human behavior. This psychological viewpoint is open to all that is true about human nature and subscribes to the need for a continual multiplication of methods and viewpoints. Van Kaam considers most theories to be differential in nature in that they focus on particular aspects or isolated profiles of behavior. In order to achieve a unified theory of behavior, there must be an integration of the numerous differential constructs. The vehicle of integration is an open on-going dialogue between the envisioned whole and the isolated parts. A comprehensive theory or total profile of behavior includes the foundational, integrational, hypothetical, creative, and communicative dimensions.

The work done by Grinker (1967), a long-time exponent of the eclectic and open system, in collaboration with anthropologists, sociologists, psychologists, economists, and biologists, represents the "general systems approach" to the comprehension of human behavior. The objective is to fashion a unified or holistic theory of man and his behavior by integrating data representing the functioning organism from the cellular level to the societal level. This interdisciplinary model seeks to interrelate and coordinate the many systems, internal and environmental, operating simultaneously in man's existence. Particular attention is directed toward the multiple transactions along the elements of a given system and between it and other systems with which it interacts.

It would be remiss not to include Gordon Allport among those who have advocated integration. Allport (1968) called himself a "polemic-eclectic" indicating that he was theoretically open, yet prepared to challenge a psychological idol. His concept of a theoretical system is "one that will allow for truth wherever found, one that encompasses the totality of human experience and does full justice to the nature of man" (p. 406). Allport was dedicated to a broad and loose program and had no desire to establish a school of psychological thought. He argued for the open system in the study of personality (Allport, 1961) and supported a "reasoned eclecticism" (Allport, 1955, 1964).

Integrative Efforts in Psychotherapy

The psychobiologic therapy or commonsense psychiatry (Lief, 1948) advanced by Adolf Meyer is generally accepted as the first serious attempt at an eclectic or integrative psychotherapy. As the term suggests, the psychobiological approach seeks an integration of the psychological (mental) and biological (physical) processes. Meyer conceived man to be fundamentally a social being who functions organismically as a body-mind/soul unity. Thus to comprehend man and his behavior, it is necessary to understand all the psycho-bio-sociologic factors. Meyer insisted on an inclusiveness regarding the 1) life history of the individual, 2) diagnosis of the clinical situation, and 3) application of techniques in the therapy process. Following an exhaustive individual, medical, and social history, a variety of techniques are used in various combinations, depending on the individual case (Billings, 1939; Sahakian, 1969).

Dollard and Miller (1950) endeavored in *Personality and Psychotherapy* to integrate the psychoanalytic concepts of Freud, the principles of learning, and the influences of culture on personality development. In their words, "the ultimate goal is to combine the vitality of psychoanalysis, the rigor of the natural-science laboratory, and the facts of culture" (p. 3). Essentially, they have subsumed Freudian thought under the rubric of reinforcement theory, or more precisely, they have interpreted or redefined Freud in learning theory terminology. As a compliment (or otherwise) to the authors, students of mine have stated that they did not understand Freud until they read Dollard and Miller.

Wolberg (1954), although sometimes identified by others as a hypnotherapist, has made a substantial effort to extract methods from the fields of psychoanalysis, psychobiology, psychiatric interviewing, case work, and therapeutic counseling and to blend these elements into an integrated and concrete methodology. His eclectic approach shows clearly that Wolberg has carefully explored the gamut of counseling theories, all of which fall into two major categories: supportive and insight therapies. Insight therapies are further divided into reeducative and reconstructive approaches. In Wolberg's approach, techniques are discriminately selected and applied; the character of a particular client and his presenting problem dictate the type of therapy.

An approach with a rather wide sweep is espoused by Blocher (1966). His *Developmental Counseling* has as its main objectives the maximizing of human freedom and human effectiveness. The system is intended to be comprehensive enough to facilitate effectively an individual's coping with all the physiological, psychological, and environmental processes characteristic of particular stages of human growth and development. A philosophical base for the developmental model is fashioned from elements of essentialism, progressivism, and existentialism. Theoretical sources examined for a synthetic system of psychotherapy include the psychoanalytic, directive counseling, client-centered, social-psychological, rational-emotive, and behavioral counseling models. This philosophico-theoretical synthesis points in the direction of seven viable models of human effectiveness: the self-actualizing person, the mature personality, the fully functioning person, the normal personality, the sound personality, the reasonable adventurer, and/or the effective personality.

Carkhuff and Berenson (1967) have provided in their "systematic eclectic stance" a praise-worthy example of integrative psychotherapy. They choose as the starting point their own well-researched central core of facilitative conditions: empathic understanding, positive regard or nonpossessive warmth, genuiness or congruence, and concreteness or specificity in expression. Around these "primary" dimensions they add systematically other "secondary" dimensions judged to be compatible with and complementary to the core conditions, and to possess the potential for constructive client gain. The secondary dimensions or "potential preferred modes of treatment" are derived from five different theoretical orientations: client-centered, existential, behavior modification, trait-and-factor, and psychoanalytic. All approaches were critically evaluated to assess strengths and weaknesses. Unique and compatible concepts, principles, methods, and procedures of each approach have been selected and incorporated in the "open, systematic, and eclectic" model.

The *Therapeutic Psychology* by Brammer and Shostrom (1968) represents another substantial integrative undertaking. They use the term "emerging eclecticism" to define their "efforts to develop a comprehensive dynamic outlook on personality structure and change as a basis for counseling practice" (p. 4). The emerging eclectic model is basically an integration of various historical and contemporary theories aimed at being both comprehensive and flexible with regard to the application of methods and techniques. The theoretical foundations are assimilated extractions of psychoanalytic, self, trait-factor, field, behavioristic-learning, process, and existential theories. The systematic blending of the humanistic, phenomenological, behavioristic, and analytic approaches provides the basis for a multidimensional approach to counseling practice. This approach provides three essentials for the theorist-practitioner: 1) a consistent theory of man and personality; 2) the basis for an intelligent selection of techniques and counseling strategies; and 3) a system that can be articulated, applied, and tested.

Bordin (1968) seeks, in his *Psychological Counseling*, to develop a general theory of psychotherapy through the integration of 1) theories emphasizing the dynamic aspects of behavior (e.g., trait-and-factor contributions, and the principles of behavioral counseling), 2) theories stressing the dynamic dimensions of behavior (orthodox Freudianism, client-centered theory, Rankian thought, and Adlerian theory), and 3) the concepts in eclectic psychobiology. Central to Bordin's position are a comprehensive theory of personality and a well-defined body of therapeutic skills and techniques to be used in the context of an interpersonal relationship.

Osipow and Walsh (1970) offer an action-oriented, developmental-based approach which results from the integration of rational theories, learning approaches, perceptual-phenomenological views, and existential perspectives. This model seeks a rapprochement of the interventionistic versus the facilitative, and the affective stage change versus the cognitive change polarities. While Osipow and Walsh prefer the interventionistic-cognitive point of view, they include the techniques and concepts of the facilitative-affective view in their integrated system. In the interventionistic-cognitive model, an openness exists with regard to counseling goals, strategies, and techniques. The uniqueness of an individual case, as disclosed through a thorough behavioral analysis, determines the *modus operandi.*

According to Woody (1971), his *Psychobehavioral Counseling and Therapy* "does not represent a theory of counseling or therapy ... but denotes a technical eclecticism, with special emphasis on the use of both conditioning and insight techniques ..." (p. 23). Another statement discloses the essence of the work: "to develop a rationale and offer guidelines for the integration of behavior therapy into insight-oriented counseling and psychotherapy" (p. ix). Woody has primarily demonstrated how client-centered counselors (really, all non-behaviorists) can complement their approach by accepting and adapting behavior modification techniques. A limited emphasis is placed on the potentially mutual complementarity of the two approaches.

Dustin and George's (1973) *Action Counseling* is another action-oriented approach stemming from the "integration of the principles of operant and classical conditioning, social learning, and client-centered therapy" (p. xiii). In the most simple terms, behavioral principles and techniques have been adapted to the client-centered relationship model and given a euphemistic label. We should note in passing that the term "action" was acquired from London (1964) who advocated a comprehensive psychotherapy via the integration of action (behavior modification) and insight (psychoanalytic and client-centered) systems. Dustin and George claim that they have achieved this integration in action counseling.

If anyone deserves the appellative "prince of the eclectics," it is Frederick Thorne. For more than thirty years, Thorne has championed eclecticism in psychotherapy. Thorne has written prolifically and each of his major works is encyclopedic in content. Thorne's thoughts are encompassed in six principal documents: *Principles of Psychological Examining* (1955), *Personality* (1961a), *Clinical Judgment* (1961b), *Tutorial Counseling* (1965), *Integrative Psychology* (1967), and *Psychological Case Handling* (1968; originally published as *Principles of Personality Counseling* in 1950).

Theories of man and the organization of human behavior are developed in *Personality* and *Integrative Psychology*. Focal in Thorne's view are "*the person*, the conscious Being, the individual running the business of life in the world" (1967, p. 1) and "the *psychological state* of the person, the status of Being in the world . . . the phenomenal (objective and subjective) 'givens' . . . of behavior . . . with the underlying factors organizing such a pattern of integration" (1967, pp. 1, 75). Thorne perceives life to be a succession of psychological states and seeks to comprehend human behavior by focusing on man *in vivo* in the stream of psychological states. In order to achieve this objective, Thorne adopts an eclectic viewpoint with a broad enough theoretical spectrum to allow for the global study of all the concomitant forces operating and interacting in the organization of behavior patterns.

Thorne's approach to therapy is outlined in the other four of the half-dozen works identified above. Systematic and nearly exhaustive consideration is given the diagnostic, etiological, and methodological factors. It is axiomatic to Thorne that: 1) no one system of therapy is equipped with an armamentarium adequate to meet the plethora of human concerns; 2) effective therapy is premised on valid diagnosis; and 3) therapeutic procedures should be based upon a rational plan suited specifically to the particular indications of each counseling situation. Thorne's attitude and objective are exemplified in the following statement:

> . . . to collect and integrate all known methods of personality counseling and psychotherapy into an eclectic system which might form the basis of standardized practice . . . to be rigidly scientific and eclectic. No priority . . . given to any theoretical viewpoint or "school" . . . to analyze the contributions of all existing schools and fit them together into an integrated system which would combine the best features of all methods. [Thorne, 1968, Vol. 1, p. vi]

Eclecticism: Pro and Con

A number of the theorists identified in the preceding discussion have adopted the term "eclectic" to define their theoretical position. Historically, eclecticism has been an approach of ill-repute but appears to be gaining a substantial reputation as a viable alternative view. Brammer and Shostrom (1968) are of the persuasion that the trend in contemporary psychotherapy is clearly toward individual variations of emerging eclecticism. Brammer (1969) contends that exclusive schools and distinctive systems of psychotherapy have passed their heyday; indeed, their days are over. Wildman and Wildman (1967) made a cross-section study of clinical psychologists in the United States and found that more practicing psychotherapists identify with eclecticism than with any other theoretical orientation.

The immediate objective is to delineate the differential attitudes toward the eclectic approach in psychotherapy. A definition will be offered in a later section.

Positive Attitudes Toward Eclecticism

At the risk of repeating in part some of the ideas exposed earlier in the historical sketch of integrative counseling, the following set of edited statements is presented as representative of the views generally held by protagonists of the eclectic model.

1. There is no single "best" kind of psychotherapy. No one theorist nor system of therapy has a monopoly on the total therapeutic truth; rather, each variant psychotherapy possesses particular aspects of the whole truth. Therefore, the eclectic viewpoint is essential to psychotherapy if the aim is to offer maximal assistance to each and every client (Wolberg, 1954).

2. The kind of therapy required is an eclecticism which is characterized by an openness and willingness to utilize any procedures which hold promise of facilitating the desired behavior change. There is no fixed preference for any system or method; the principle of practical necessity takes precedence over orthodoxy (Marzolf, 1956).

3. The surest way to lose truth is to operate with the pretense of being already in full possession of it. As desirable and necessary as particular systems might be, the only way to comprehend the nature of man and the human situation is by a reasoned and systematic eclecticism marked by a conceptual and theoretical openness. A comprehensive metatheory is preferred to a plurality of dogmatized and separatistic particularisms (Allport, 1955; 1964).

4. The enormous array of clinical concerns presented by clients necessitates differential diagnoses and differential choices of therapeutic methods. The only justifiable grounds for a psychotherapist to use only one method would be a practice restricted to a clientele with the same type of problem. The one-method counselor, the screwdriver mechanic, and the penicillin physician are equally unscientific, unprofessional, unethical, and immoral. It is time to call for a moratorium on the one-method counselor (Callis, 1960).

5. All theories and theorists (indeed, all counselors and therapists) are eclectic in the sense that they have borrowed certain ideas, concepts, and principles from someone else. It would be a gross mistake to assume that any one counseling approach is replete with the full range of human development and experience. Firm and passionate loyalty to a particular theory and/or theorist should be discouraged at all stages of one's professional development (Williamson, 1965).

6. Man, as a free being, cannot be confined to a monolithic system. In order to assist the client toward effective living, the therapist must select from many systems those elements which promise to be most useful in given situations. Empirical data suggest that the most effective approach is an open-ended, systematic, eclectic model fashioned around a central core of facilitative conditions and complemented with a variety of techniques derived from several theoretical orientations (Carkhuff and Berenson, 1967).

7. A psychotherapist can hardly afford to ignore any technique proven to be effective, regardless of its theoretical origin. The counselor-therapist who maintains a strict adherence to a particular school of thought arbitrarily excludes from his repertoire many effective procedures. Technical eclecticism has decided potential to enrich the practitioner's therapeutic effectiveness without jeopardizing his theoretical position (Lazarus, 1967).

8. An individualized emerging eclecticism consisting of a comprehensive view of personality structure and change and a multidimensional approach to psychotherapy provides best a) a consistent and personally satisfying frame of reference for the therapist and b) an adequately broad base for assisting clients with diverse problems and concerns (Brammer and Shostrom, 1968).

9. Eclecticism, a blending of many techniques to serve best the needs of clients at various stages or phases in the therapy process, is the prerequisite for complete or total psychotherapy. Therapy must match the needs of the particular client if it is to be genuinely effective (affecting the total personality, or as much of it as possible, through the utilization of a variety of approaches), and sectarianism unavoidably limits therapeutic effectiveness (Slavson, 1970).

Criticism of Eclecticism

The psychoanalytic model and the eclectic approach have been the most and second most negatively criticized systems of psychotherapy, respectively. Traditionalists have denounced eclecticism for many years. There is reason to speculate that the critical attacks have come more from a defensive posture than otherwise. That which dares to move beyond the status quo poses as a threat to the orthodox mind. The following discussion focuses on the lines of attack on the eclectic outlook.

1. Boring (1929) perceived eclectics to be middle-of-the-road nonentities who steal ideas from original thinkers, run off with their booty and prepare sophomoric textbooks which are written from no established point of view and in defense of nothing. To make matters worse, it is the eclectic thief who gets credit rather than the originator.

2. "Goethe decried namby-pamby eclecticism where directionless eclectics are comparable to jackdaws who aimlessly carry anything and everything to their nests" (Allport, 1964, p. 27).

Patterson (1959), a benevolent relationship therapist, has spotted what he considers to be four basic weaknesses in the eclectic approach:

3. Too much emphasis is placed on the selection and application of techniques rather than on attitudes and feelings of the counselor or therapist;

4. The approach is too manipulative to be of optimal benefit to the client;

5. Essentially, eclecticism is a bag-of-tricks and trial-and-error approach which has no adequate information regarding the criteria to govern what techniques to use when and with what clients; and

6. The eclectic approach has no general principles of counseling and lacks a logical rationale; it is simply a random collection of techniques held together in a loose and nonsystematic fashion.

7. Although an ardent eclectic himself, Brammer (1969) is critical, and rightly so, of those individuals who "choose bits and pieces . . . indiscriminately . . . from a wide spectrum of counseling theories and methods . . . and concoct a hodgepodge of contradictory assumptions and incompatible techniques" (pp. 192, 193).

Thorne (1973a, 1973b), the chief spokesman for the eclectic position, has ferreted out other critical attacks on eclecticism:

8. Eclectics are confused and indecisive people who are unable to choose between competing and conflicting systems of psychotherapy.

9. Eclecticism is really a form of professional nihilism charac-

terized by disillusioned psychotherapists wandering aimlessly and experimenting undiscerningly and haplessly with novel methods.

10. Eclecticism is typically a "blind, willy-nilly cookbook" therapy.

11. Eclecticism is a harbor for individuals who are either too lazy or inept to master one of the major systems of therapy.

12. The eclectic is a jack-of-all-trades and master of none.

13. Eclectics tend to have the unrealistic belief that they can become all things to all people. Thus their ambition exceeds their ability to perform.

14. The eclectic practitioner is more of a technician, who is preoccupied with the mechanical application of an armamentarium of methods, than a personal and discerning therapist.

15. The training of eclectic counselors and psychotherapists is generally sketchy and superficial; they touch on everything but comprehend nothing.

16. Eclecticism has failed to develop a body of knowledge that can be empirically tested to determine its therapeutic effectiveness.

17. To claim to be eclectic is a preposterous notion; it is impossible for an individual to investigate exhaustively all known systems of therapy and create a comprehensive superordinate synthesis.

The chore of addressing and refuting these charges is left for the reader to perform. May it suffice to say that a) most of the charges are gross and unfounded generalizations, b) many of the charges are equally applicable to all approaches to psychotherapy, and c) a few of the criticisms are fair descriptions of historical eclecticism.

Definitions and Distinctions

A number of terms need to be defined and distinguished before we proceed with the development of the thesis. These terms have received their share of semantic workouts in the past, but it is desired that the reader understand the meaning the terms carry in this context.

Eclectic and Eclecticism

The etymological source of these two nounal cognates is the Greek verbal root *eklego,* a composite of *ek* (from or out of) and *lego* (to pick, choose or select). Eclectic means then, literally, to pick out or to select from. The following example represents quite typically the dictionary definitions of eclectic: "Selecting what appears to be best in various doctrines, methods, or styles" (*Webster's Seventh*

New Collegiate Dictionary). Hopke (1968), a counselor educator, fails to advance the understanding of the concept when he writes: "Eclectic means to select; to choose appropriate doctrines or methods from various sources or systems" (p. 121). Similarly, "Eclectic counseling is counseling that is based upon different methods, concepts, and techniques selected from different schools of thought" (Hopke, p. 121). As Brammer (1969) poignantly observes, "This literal definition fitted counseling eclecticism of past decades quite well; but reconstitution of the concept is very much needed today" (p. 192).

The definition developed by English and English (1958) meets the demands of the hour and reflects the position delineated herein:

> Eclecticism . . . in theoretical system building, has reference to the selection and orderly combination of compatible features from diverse sources, sometimes from otherwise incompatible theories and systems; the effort to find valid elements in all doctrines or theories and to combine them into a harmonious whole. The resulting system is open to constant revision even in its major outlines . . . Eclecticism is to be distinguished from unsystematic and uncritical combination, for which the name is syncretism. The eclectic . . . a systematizer . . . seeks as much consistency and order as is currently possible; but he is unwilling to sacrifice conceptualizations that put meaning into a wide range of facts for the sake of what he is apt to think of as a premature and unworkable over-all systematization. The formalist thus finds the eclectic's formulation too loose and uncritical. For his part, the eclectic finds formalism and schools too dogmatic and rigid, too much inclined to reject, if not facts, at least helpful conceptualizations of fact. [p. 168]

It is appropriate to consider counseling eclecticism to be comprised of the personal-theoretical and technical domains. *Personal-theoretical eclecticism* has to do with the theorist's personal formulation of a) the nature of man, b) a theory of personality, c) a theory of disordered or disruptive behavior, and d) a theory of behavior change. *Technical eclecticism* has reference to the systematization of a body of methods, techniques, procedures, and strategies to be employed in the therapeutic setting to effect change in personality and behavior. A blending of the two domains results in a comprehensive psychotherapy.

Integration

The terms eclecticism and integration can be, and most often are, used synonymously when talking about the convergence of psychotherapies. But to confound the two concepts is likely to result in the loss of certain features with significant import.

The word integration stems from the Latin verb *integrare* which means to make whole or to form into a whole. Again, English and English (1958) provide definitional data strategic to this discourse:

> *Integrate* . . . to bring parts together into a whole or totality; to bind firmly together into a functioning whole . . . *Integration* . . . the process (or result) of bringing together and unifying parts into a whole; the production of units of a higher order. [p. 267]

Integration is superordinate in relation to eclecticism. Integration is the systematic putting-together process, while eclecticism is essentially the discriminate searching-gathering-collating process. The two processes (and terms) are Siamese twins and are equally indispensable to theory building. When I say that I am an integrationist, it is to be assumed that I am first an eclectic. Hence the rationale for Integrative rather than Eclectic in the title of this work.

Counseling and/or Psychotherapy

Virtually every major work, as well as scores of articles and essays, on counseling and psychotherapy devotes a number of pages to the question: Are counseling and psychotherapy distinct disciplines or are they synonyms for the same professional function? A rehashing of the debate is unwarranted here. On the basis of the etymology of the two concepts, psychotherapy (healing of the mind, soul, or life) is preferred by the writer over counseling (consulting or giving advice). But the practical aspect does not allow for such an easy bifurcation. Any difference that might exist between counseling and psychotherapy appears to be more quantitative than qualitative. Therefore, the most reasonable position to take on this issue is the one exemplified in the assertion that:

> There are no essential differences between counseling and psychotherapy in the nature of the relationship, in the process, in the methods or techniques, in goals or outcomes (broadly conceived), or even in the kinds of clients involved. For convenience, or for practical or political reasons, counseling often refers to work with less seriously disturbed clients or with clients who have rather specific problems with less accompanying general personality disturbance, usually in a nonmedical setting; while psychotherapy refers to work with more seriously disturbed clients, usually in a medical setting. [Patterson, 1973, p. xiv]

We elect to view counseling and psychotherapy as arbitrary and overlapping points on a continuum with no clear indication of where counseling ends and psychotherapy begins. Therefore, the terms counseling and psychotherapy are used interchangeably in this treatise.

Integrative Counseling and Psychotherapy

A definition is offered but with no pretense of being novel. The ideas of a number of other theorists, particularly Robert Carkhuff and Bernard Berenson, are reflected in the statement presented here.

Integrative counseling and psychotherapy is an attempt to develop a comprehensive and multidimensional approach to counseling and psychotherapy by investigating and blending the unique contributions of a wide variety of existing theories and methods into an integrated system which is open, yet scientific and systematic. Central to this system are: 1) well-articulated conceptualizations of a) the nature of man, b) the structure and development of the healthy personality, c) the nature of disordered behavior, and d) a theory of behavior change; 2) a core of interpersonal relationship skills and attitudes conducive to therapeutic change; and 3) an armamentarium of methods, techniques, procedures, and strategies adequate to assist a cross-section of clients with diverse problems and concerns.

This statement represents in kernel form the content to be developed in the remainder of this volume.

Guidelines for Integration

There appear to be only three alternative avenues to follow in building a personal theory of counseling and psychotherapy. One can resort to the strategy of denial and repress data that do not agree with a preferred partial model. Or one can elect to take the piecemeal eclectic route and carry elements of all theories indiscriminately into a namby-pamby jackdaw nest. Or one can struggle systematically for a comprehensive system that incorporates and integrates all valid concepts, principles, and methods regardless of their theoretical origin (Allport, 1964).

This final section of the chapter seeks to outline some basic steps to follow in the process of systematic integration. The outline is intended to reflect a semblance of the orderliness that should be observed in the logical and chronological development of a system. The steps in the process are not discrete and exclusive, rather they are mutually interdependent. The sketchy treatment given the content here will be supplemented with detailed discussions in succeeding chapters.

1. *Exploration and Observation*

Foundational to the scientific process of theory building is an inquisitive and open mind. The eclectic integrationist is characterized by intellectual and theoretical openness, and he pursues truth wherever found. His active exploration and observation lead him into many fields of knowledge and provide him with data adequate for constructing both a personally satisfying world view and a comprehensive theoretical framework.

A. *Knowledge of Self.* A great many counselor-psychotherapists (this one included) believe that, since counseling-psychotherapy is an interpersonal relationship, the personality of the counselor-therapist is just as important, if not more important, as any other aspect of the counseling process. Thus, the building of a counseling theory should begin with self-exploration. Knowledge of self includes, among other factors, awareness of one's values, needs, attitudes, interests, priorities, assets, and limitations.

B. *An Articulated Philosophy of Life.* Inextricably bound to one's view of self is his conception of man and the universe. If counseling is a way of life (this writer and others — e.g., Boy & Pine, 1968, and Carkhuff & Berenson, 1967 — understand counseling to be just that), then it behooves the counselor-therapist to be in possession of an integrated world view. The ideological determinants of the theorist's view of life influence critically all other aspects of theory construction.

C. *A Psychology of Human Development and Behavior.* Strategic to the development of an integrative psychotherapy are the contributions of diverse schools of thought regarding the structure and development of the healthy personality, the nature of personality disorder, and theory of behavioral change. An extensive investigation of this wide area of human knowledge is imperative.

D. *Interpersonal Relationship Skills.* To be thoroughly explored, both academically and experientially, are those interpersonal parameters and conditions proven necessary and/or conducive to therapeutic change or gain. Particular attention should be devoted to the theorist's own style of interacting with and relating to other people.

E. *Therapeutic Methods.* The eclectic integrationist must become acquainted, via every means possible, with the multitude of differential modes of therapy. No school of psychotherapy thought is to be bypassed; the desirability of a therapeutic method should not be determined in any way by the source of its origination. A major criterion should be: Has the technique been tested and shown to be effective? The mere existence of a method warrants neither a blind acceptance nor a biased rejection of it.

2. *Selection and Assimilation*

The exploring-observing process simply provides the building blocks for a theory. The next scientific procedures are the discriminate selection of appropriate data and the systematic assimilation of the evidence. Success at this stage consists of 1) a comprehension of self and a workable world view around which 2) a psychology of human development and behavior is erected, and supplemented with 3) a tentative system of therapy involving a core of facilitative conditions complemented with a variety of therapeutic methods.

Assuming a constancy of intellectual and theoretical openness and a devotion to systematization, three principal criteria mark the selecting-assimilating process: data are to be compatible with the personality and world view of theorist; data should be internally consistent; and data must be empirically sound.

3. *Experimentation*

The tentative formulations made at the selective-assimilative stage are at best untested hypotheses. The hypothesized system must be put to empirical test in reality in order to determine: 1) compatibility between the personal-philosophic-theoretical tenets and the technical-procedural aspects; 2) over-all consistency; and 3) practical effectiveness. A concept, principle, or method is not one's own until he has "tried it on for proper fit."

The experimental process discussed here has particular reference to experiential learning and supervised practica at the pre-service stage of professional development. However, the same empiric attitude should hold throughout life.

4. *Integration*

The cumulative results of the exploratory, observational, selective, assimilative, and experimental processes combine to form an integrated and well-articulated system of counseling and psychotherapy. The system is comprehensive and multidimensional; it is open, yet systematic, consistent, and empirically sound; it is a definitive position that is flexible and "fits" the personality and world view of the theorist.

A diagram is provided in Figure 1 to show the profile of the basic structure of the integrative theory of counseling and psychotherapy.

FIGURE 1

A Profile of the Basic Structure of Integrative Theory

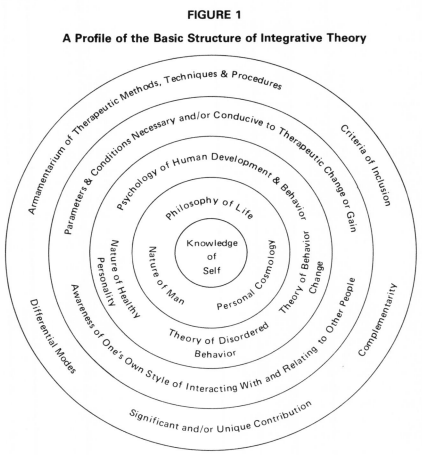

5. *Application*

Just as the proof of the pudding is in the eating, the veracity of a therapy system is demonstrated in its consistent effectiveness in the real world. Repeated application and testing of the theory discloses the need for continual revision, updating, and modification to insure a truly scientific posture and maximal effectiveness. Indubitably, the nitty-gritty of practical experience is the crucible in which authentic integration is forged into formality and solidarity.

6. *Re (Neo) integration*

The eclectic integrationist has full awareness that his system is ever temporary. At no time can he pretend to be in possession of the final truth, nor does he dare to present a closed system. Rather, he actively seeks new truth to be incorporated and integrated into his emerging system. Although the counselor-therapist's personal-philosophic-theoretical outlook remains fairly constant, he must struggle to blend in new concepts, methods, and procedures. In essence, the building of an integrative theory is a life-long process in which the counselor-therapist is in the process of becoming adjunct to a forward-moving system.

The integrative process is summarized schematically in Figure 2, on the following page.

24 / *Integrative Counseling and Psychotherapy*

FIGURE 2

A Schematic Outline of the Integrative Process

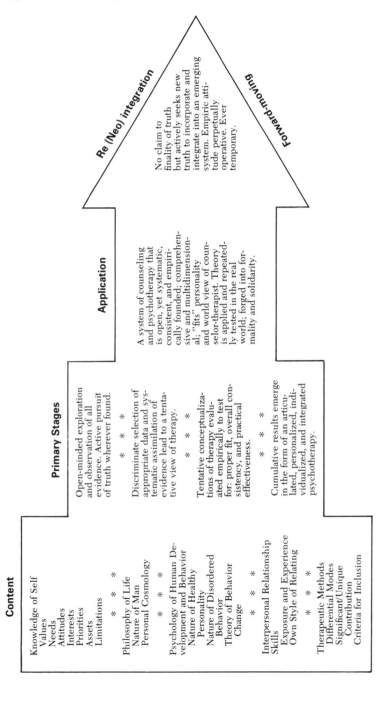

Content

Knowledge of Self
Values
Needs
Attitudes
Interests
Priorities
Assets
Limitations

* *
* *

Philosophy of Life
Nature of Man
Personal Cosmology

* *
* *

Psychology of Human Development and Behavior
Nature of Healthy Personality
Nature of Disordered Behavior
Theory of Behavior Change

* *
* *

Interpersonal Relationship Skills
Exposure and Experience
Own Style of Relating

* *
* *

Therapeutic Methods
Differential Modes
Significant/Unique Contribution
Criteria for Inclusion

Primary Stages

Open-minded exploration and observation of all evidence. Active pursuit of truth wherever found.

* * *

Discriminate selection of appropriate data and systematic assimilation of evidence lead to a tentative view of therapy.

* * *

Tentative conceptualizations of therapy evaluated empirically to test for: proper fit, overall consistency, and practical effectiveness.

* * *

Cumulative results emerge in the form of an articulated, personalized, individualized, and integrated psychotherapy.

Application

A system of counseling and psychotherapy that is open, yet systematic, consistent, and empirically founded; comprehensive and multidimensional; "fits" personality and world view of counselor-therapist. Theory is applied and repeatedly tested in the real world; forged into formality and solidarity.

Re (Neo) integration

Forward-moving

No claim to finality of truth but actively seeks new truth to incorporate and integrate into an emerging system. Empiric attitude perpetually operative. Ever temporary.

2

Philosophic-Theoretical Groundwork

This chapter purports to formulate a philosophic-theoretical base for an integrative psychotherapy. The conceptualizations posited here represent the personal position of the writer and are not intended in any measure to be prescriptive for others. But should my effort make the task of building a counseling theory a little easier for those struggling with the problems of integration, then a specific goal of this work will be accomplished. In other words, the personalized approach delineated in this volume, this chapter in particular, could serve no greater purpose than being a facilitative model to the reader.

The limitations imposed by the nature of a monograph preclude an exhaustive discussion of pertinent knowledge. Consequently, the philosophical and theoretical conceptions offered below are essential outlines of more expansive ideas. Be this as it may, an attempt will be made to establish definitive positions on: 1) the nature of man, 2) a personal cosmology, 3) a psychology of human development and behavior, and 4) a theory of behavior modification or therapy.

Again, no claim is made to originality. Every idea mentioned here has been conceived by someone, in some form, at some time prior to the existence of this manuscript. However, since these conceptions constitute significant segments of "my" phenomenal field, "I" proudly and courageously claim them as "mine." A sincere and constant effort will be made to give credit where credit is due; the writer is free of any desire to engage in the "eclectic thievery" strongly deplored by Boring (1929).

Hopefully, a straight-forward presentation will materialize, since there appears to be little, if any, virtue in theoretical and philosophical diplomacy or fence-straddling. With this perspective in mind, let's get on with "operation candor."

Toward Theoretical Holism

A prerequisite to integrative theory is having the capacity to transcend the "either/or mentality" which has been quite prevalent among psychologists and psychotherapists. Of weighty concern to the advocate of integrative eclecticism is the matter of wholeness in truth. An inflexible attachment to philosophic-theoretical particularism prohibits integrative enterprise. But, the particularistic outlook has produced, in the larger part, extant psychological knowledge. The challenge facing the integrationist is basically this: He, with a mind-set different from that which formulated existing truth, must make united sense out of the isolated parts and fragments.

It should be advantageous to focus on some of the tendencies of rigid particularism before making any attempts toward holistic reconstruction. After briefly discussing each of four consequential propensities of "either/or" thinking, a mode of attitudinal transcendence will be suggested.

Reductionism

A comprehension of the human organism rests on the harmonious blending of four basic meaning constructs: The *substance construct* is necessary to define the intrinsic essence or nature of man; the *impetus construct* is required to account for the energizing and motivating forces in human behavior; the *pattern construct* facilitates the understanding of the structure and organization of personality and behavior; and the *intentional construct* provides a basis for apprehending the purposiveness in human behavior (Rychlak, 1973). Rather than seeing these constructs in constellation, the tendency has been to reduce man and behavior to a single construct (at best two constructs) and to regard this particularized model as the total truth. This amounts to what Frankl (1969) describes as a "pseudoscientific approach which disregards and ignores the humanness of phenomena by making them into mere epiphenomena, more specifically, by reducing them to subhuman phenomena" (p. 18). Illustrative examples of reductionism are a) Freud's (1970) insistence that the master determinant of behavior is the pleasure (sex) principle, b) Skinner's (1971) defining man as a mere physical organism environmentally determined or conditioned, and c) the attempt by Ellis (1973) to account for the total of human disturbance on the grounds of magical or irrational thinking.

Our inability to apprehend the whole of reality or truth at once makes the differential or particular constructs necessary, but these isolated profiles of the nature of man and behavior must be integrated in order to achieve a comprehensive theory (van Kaam, 1966).

Dualism

Dogmatic reductionism (particularism) leads to a polarization of the truth. The tendency, paradoxically, is to create dualisms or bipolarities in which the *truth* is on one side (your position) and the *error* or non-truth on the other side (your "opponent's" position). James (1907) has provided a paradigm into which a series of dualisms can be fitted.

THE TENDER-MINDED VERSUS THE TOUGH-MINDED

Rationalism (going by 'principles')	Empiricism (going by 'facts')
A Priori Reasoning	A Posteriori Reasoning
Intellect	Sensations
Idealism	Materialism
Optimism	Pessimism
Pro-religion	Anti-religion
Free-will/Freedom	Fatalism/Determinism
Holism/Monism	Particularism/Pluralism
Dogmatism/Strong Affirmations	Scepticism/Tentativeness
Affect	Cognition
Metaphysical	Physical
Mind/Consciousness	Body/Tangibleness
Unconscious Processes	Conscious Processes
Insight	Action
Present & Future	Past & Present
Support	Manipulation
Humanism	Behaviorism
Non-directive	Directive

The list could be extended indefinitely, but it is sufficient to illustrate the point as it stands. The two columns of concepts are not at all mutually exclusive. Rather, the concepts are mutually dependent; only one-half of the truth is represented on either side of the bipolar dyads. The whole truth resides in the integrality of the partial truths of both sides.

Exclusionism

Theoretical particularism manifests itself in another manner which we have already referred to as the "strategy of denial." Evidence that does not fit or agree with a preferred partial model is arbitrarily rejected. In each and every reductionistic theory, only certain prescribed constructs belong to its particular frame of reference which necessarily excludes all other constructs. Thus, differential or partial theories are all marked by mutual exclusion.

Exclusiveness

The fourth and most ostentatious tendency of the either/or mentality is to fashion a system around a limited number of constructs and to commercialize it as an exclusive panacea. This attitude was sufficiently addressed in Chapter 1 under the rubric of "denominational psychotherapy." We would add that the drift toward exclusiveness is communicated most vividly in the founding of institutes to propagate the "gospel truth" of exclusive systems — The Institute for Advanced Study in Rational [-Emotive] Psychotherapy, Alfred Adler Institute, Institute for Transactional Analysis, Institute for Reality Therapy, Institute of C. G. Jung Association for Analytical Psychology, etc., etc.

Transcending the Either/Or Mentality

In order to integrate differential systems, there must be an attitude that transcends the tendencies of dichotomous thinking. In another place (Smith, 1973), *synergistic love* has been suggested as the necessary condition for transcending the either/or mentality.

If love can be conceived as a basic attitude toward life (devotion to the welfare of mankind rather than to the defense of an ideology or theoretical system) that is demonstrated through creative and purposeful action, then it follows that love has unlimited potential as a synergistic force in forming a holistic view of man and behavior from the constructs derived from a variety of differential theories.

O'Neill and O'Neill (1972) define synergy as the "dynamic process that occurs when the combined action of two or more things produce a more beneficial and greater effect or result than the sum of their separate individual actions" (p. 260). Maslow (1965) has described synergy as being the transcendence of dichotomous either/or thinking and equates such a process with love.

Picking up Maslow's (1965) definition of synergy as the resolution of the dichotomy between selfishness and altruism, the following paraphrastic rendition is offered as a plausible mode of overcoming the mutual exclusiveness of differential systems. The humanism versus behaviorism polarity is illustrated in the example, but the paradigm is equally applicable to all philosophic-theoretical dualisms.

Synergistic love can be defined as the resolution of the dichotomy between humanism and behaviorism. The theoretical approaches humanism and behaviorism, as mutually exclusive, have become meaningless. The two approaches to psychotherapy have fused together. My practice of psychotherapy is neither humanistic exclusively nor behavioral exclusively; my personal/professional behavior is both humanistic and behavioristic simultaneously. My actions, my attitudes, my life are synergic. One might say it means in certain respects different systems can be treated as if they are not so different, as if they are one, as if they are pooled, or lumped, or fused, or integrated into a new kind of system which is superordinate and includes them both, fusing their separate strengths. Thus the application of synergistic love represents the transcendence of the dichotomous two-valued orientation of polarizing into either humanism and behaviorism.

Synergistic love will be the motivating force behind the effort to be made in the residuum of this volume to achieve a) holism in philosophical and theoretical conceptualizations and b) comprehensiveness and multidimensionality in psychotherapeutic practice.

A Concept of Man

The principle determinant of a personal and bona fide approach to counseling and psychotherapy is without a doubt the counselor-therapist's conception of man. If man is conceived as being largely determined by unconscious dynamics, then an analytical system will be designed to effect insight into the psyche (Freud). When man is conceptualized as a verbal and rational animal, a highly cognitive and rational re-educative system of therapy follows (Ellis). Should man be viewed as having intrinsic goodness, worth and dignity, a psychotherapy stressing relationship parameters emerges (Rogers). This cause and effect pattern is evidenced consistently in all systems of therapy.

Two objectives are in mind for this section. In the first place, a brief survey will be made of the major conceptualizations of the nature of man. Secondly, in harmony with a basic theme of the monograph, the writer will express his personal view of man with a conception of the cosmos.

Varied Conceptions of Man

The countless variations in anthropological conceptualizations can be discussed parsimoniously under the four central theories suggested by Tweedie (1961).

The Mechanical Man

This view, which originated in pre-Socratic Greek thought and continues to this day, considers man as a purely physical entity whose existence stems from the chance linkage of physical particles which make up the atomic universe — he is an organized body of matter among an innumerable quantity of more or less similar material bodies. Man is essentially a machine whose behavior conforms to the general physical laws of nature. Aspects of behavior which lack rigid empirical validation are considered spurious in nature and must be rejected. As Allport (1962) has observed, man, in this model, is simply a reactive organism no different in kind from a monkey, dog, or pigeon whose behavior is to be studied biologically, behaviorally and mathematically in predictable terms. The mechanical view presents man as a robot (Ford & Urban, 1963) whose present situation is completely determined in his past by the environmental contingencies of survival and reinforcement. This conception of man is espoused by the psychologists and psychotherapists who operate from the behavioristic stance.

The Phylogenetic Man

Man is conceived in this naturalistic model as a complex biological organism who, through the evolutionary process, emerged from inanimate matter. The reality of his being alive renders man an inexplicable enigma according to the rules and principles of physical science. This view, popularized by Darwin, ascribes to man the regal position over the kingdom of all living things on the account of his self-consciousness and rationality. However, man's noblest aspirations and achievements are reduced to cellular activity; and, his social behavior and rational beingness are described as accidental results of biological instincts, needs, motives, and drives. Thus, man is a reactive being in depth who differs from the mechanical man only in the depth dimension (Allport, 1962). In the mechanical view, man is the victim of his external environment; in the phylogenetic view, he is the victim of his internal environment. The phylogenetic conception of man is assumed by Freudian psychoanalysis and cognate systems.

Man, the Rational Animal

The rational or "classical" view of man has its roots in the thoughts of Socrates, Plato, and Aristotle. Man is seen as unique in the animal world due to his rational faculties. The rational part of man — the mind — is the unifying principle and is identified with the creative and ordering principle of the universe. The rational or classical view posits an anthropologic dualism in which an essentially good rational and immortal soul/mind is imprisoned in a base body plagued by passions and drives. Man expresses his true nature or essence only when he is thinking to attain rational ends. Man's defects and problems stem from ignorance and irrationality and are removed through rational thinking. The modern scientific viewpoint rules out the metaphysical concept of an immortal soul or mind, limiting anthropological knowledge to empirically derived evidence. Nevertheless, a scientific-based rational view of man exists in a goodly proportion today; e.g., the anthropologic image in the rational-emotive psychotherapy of Ellis.

Man in the Image of God

This view, derived from the Hebraic-Christian tradition, conceives man as the creature of a personal Deity, and in some definite but limited way is made in the image of God. The uniqueness of man — intellectual creativity, intrinsic worth and nobility, capacity for self-transcendence, ability and freedom to make choices — stems from his being in the likeness of God. According to this view, man is a unity of mind , body, and spirit. Furthermore, man is a part of nature but distinct from mere animal existence.

The failure of metaphysical phenomena to attain scientific respectability, and the repressive elements in Reformation and Puritan theology regarding the nature of man, have caused contemporary psychology and psychotherapy to repudiate the Biblical view of man. The tendency has been to emphasize the individuality, self-sufficiency, naturalness, and rationality of man who has "come of age" and does not need the aid of the supernatural (Beck, 1963; Kemp, 1967). But, admittedly or unadmittedly, the majority of the existential-phenomenological approaches to counseling and psychotherapy depend upon the Hebraic-Christian tradition for their basic conceptualizations of the essential nature of the human being.

Personal Views of the Universe and Man

The following discourse is an honest, perhaps courageous, attempt to define my conceptions of man and the universe in which he resides. In essence it is an exposition of how I perceive myself and my world. But it also represents the world view I bring into all my interpersonal relationships. Too, it is the philosophical foundation upon which I have erected, and am continually perfecting, an individualized approach to counseling and psychotherapy. More tersely, these concepts provide *for me* an answer to the meaning of human existence. The immediate concern then is not with personality and behavior — these factors will be explored in succeeding sections — rather, it is with the how, the what, the where, and the why of man. To pretend a psychotherapy without a satisfactory answer to these questions would be playing the ostrich.

A Personal Cosmology

Any conceptualization of the universe can be placed accurately in one of four major categorizations: Personal-Theistic, Impersonal-Deistic, Social-Agnostic, or Nonpersonal-Atheistic. The *Personal-Theistic* view conceives the universe as an orderly system designed by an omniscient and omnipotent Creator who is personal, friendly, and approachable. A "Grand Plan" is built into the universe, and God, according to the principles and laws He has established in nature, benevolently guides or executes the plan. God has particular love and concern for man. The *Impersonal-Deistic* view holds that a supernatural or creative force created the world and man and then chose to abandon permanently the total creation. A vast, impersonal principle (natural law) operates throughout the universe, but is indifferent to man. The *Social-Agnostic* view maintains that metaphysical questions regarding the origin of man and the universe and the existence of God or a Supreme Being are purely academic and that there is no way of knowing or finding out the answers. Even if we knew the answer, the quality of life would be little affected. Man is adequately enlightened and, if given the opportunity, possesses self-sufficiency enough to manage his own affairs without the help of a Deity. Social relationships and culture are the significant elements in an individual's universe, and the big concern is to build a society filled with justice, equality, and humanitarianism. The *Nonpersonal-Atheistic* cosmology postulates that the universe can be described best as a machine. Both man and nature are the results of cause and effect determinism. There is no God or supernatural force, nor is there any need for one; natural law adequately accounts for everything.

The first question to be answered in arriving at a personal cosmology has to do with origin: Did the universe evolve into its present state from inanimate and pre-existent matter, or was it effected by some creative Being? As a professor once challenged us in an introductory course in physical anthropology, it's a matter of "faith" whichever route you take. Precisely, which is more credible, the eternality of matter or a pre-existent Creator? It is inconceivable that cause and effect determinism premised on the chance factor could produce the splendor, the complex uniformity and harmony, the vast multiplicity, and the enormous resourcefulness observed in both the entire macrocosm and the microcosm of the single human being. For this reason, among others, the *Personal-Theistic* view is the most plausible one to me.

Central in my concept of the universe is a God who exists eternally as a Personal Being. He possesses infinite intelligence and power, yet He is kind, gentle, and compassionate. Although He is characterized by absolute goodness, God has the capacity to express constructive anger. His being a Person makes interpersonal relationships between God and man both feasible and desirable. Relationships with God are established on the same bases as are all other person-to-person relationships — love, trust and commitment. It is easy to entertain the thought that the God-man relationship is the prototype of all interpersonal relationships.

I conceive the universe as the best of all possible cosmic systems. It was designed, formed, and established by the infinite genius of God. Though distinct from and transcendent to the universe, God is personally and immanently involved in the sustenance of it. The cosmos is engineered for maximal efficiency and beauty. From the moment of creation the universe was complete, yet filled with mysteries and hidden secrets enough to challenge the curious and creative mind of man for countless millennia. Not only is the universe of a definite design, it exists for a purpose — much like the purpose for which you and I design and build a home or some other creative project — to give the Creator exuberant pleasure *and* to be a source of intense and lasting enjoyment for all who share or experience it. Man is focal in both the design and plan of the universe. The universe, the earth in particular, was fashioned for man and man has a regal position in it. The laws and principles built into the cosmos, rather than being the forces that have determined man, are to be discovered by man and used ingeniously to make the world productive for him and to enhance his existence. When God actualized Himself in the creation of the world and man, He included in the overall design ample provision for man to be self-actualizing. Thus, the universe as a planned system does *not* suggest, as many critics of the theistic model are prone to argue, a willful despot making all the decisions and reducing man to the status of robot. Rather, it is the best of all possible designs in which man can be fully human and maximize his potential.

Turning from the ontological nature of the universe to the social context of human existence, a participant democracy is posited as the form of societal structure most conducive to optimal development of human potential. *Only* in a community of sharing fellows who practice the principles of equality, freedom, and justice can the individuality and dignity of the human being be fostered.

A Personal View of Man

Adoption of a personal-theistic cosmology precludes all anthropologic conceptions except the "man-in-the-image-of-God" view — or does it? Cosmological philosophies are of such great polarity that a particularistic stance is virtually unavoidable when establishing a personal view. Fortunately, the views of man, though dichotomous, are less so than are cosmologies. The unique contributions of each of the conceptions of man, which were reviewed earlier, are needed in the construction of a complete anthropology. To posit a universe of theistic design necessarily includes man as a creature of God, but this is an inclusive, rather than exclusive, concept of man.

Man, as a creature of God, exists and functions as a holistic organism. He is a unity of *soma* (body), *psyche* (soul or reflective mind), *nous* (reason or active mind), and *pneuma* (spirit). Somatically, man is essentially animal and behaves much like any other biological organism. Even many of the elemental psychical phenomena surrounding man are little different from those characteristic of animal behavior. In his chemistry, physics, and biology, man is one with nature. But when we enter the higher mental or psychic processes and the pneumatic or spiritual dimensions, phenomena unique to man are observed. (Among all biological creatures man alone has *nous* and *pneuma*.) Man is a creature of nature *but* he is very much more than a mere biological organism — man is uniquely a human being, indeed, a rational and spiritual being.

How do we account for the uniqueness of man? Not on the basis of the evolutionary hypothesis which posits man as the most advanced species in the phylogenetic spectrum; rather, on the basis of man's being in the image of God. Is it not really preposterous to think that unique *Homo Sapiens* could be produced through the natural and self-perpetuating process of cause-and-effect determinism? A more tenable position is this: When God created man, He shared with or invested in man His personal attributes of intelligence, power, volition, creativeness, nobility, dignity, worth, freedom, sense of personhood, immortality, and capacity for transcendence. Human personhood is derived from the personhood of God, not from eternal ionized gaseous atoms, and herein lies the essence of man.

I further conceive man as essentially free. Man is endowed with the ability and the freedom to plan, to decide, to act, and to become. He is determined by neither his past, present, nor future. There are many environmental limitations, internal and external, with which he must struggle and/or accept, but the real choices, not illusions, which man can make determine to a large extent the quality of his life. Biology and environment *a man* do not make — man can transcend mundane and programmed existence.

Regarding the matter of good or evil in man, I have struggled to believe as Carl Rogers (1961) does that man is basically good. But honest analyses of my own selfish tendencies, the constant effort required to help my children learn altruism, the history of wars, the universality of lock and key, social-political situations as Watergate, and greed phenomena such as those surrounding the "energy crisis" make believing difficult. Nor is it easy to believe that man is born good and society corrupts him. The answer to the presence of evil in the world lies somewhere between the poles of man is good and man is evil. Thus, I see man as possessing the potential for both good and evil and a task in life is to seek good and learn to reject or control those behaviors which are destructive. In other words, man has the potential to behave either in a truly humane manner or in animalistic fashion. Whether each of the propensities is innate or acquired cannot be clearly decided. Perhaps the only reasonable answer is that some of the good and some of the bad in man are there due to both inheritance and learning.

Regardless of the quality of his behavior and existential situation, man retains, intrinsically and indelibly, his personhood marked by nobility, worth, creative intelligence, volition, and the potential for transcendence. These are the differentiating characteristics of *Homo in imagine Dei*. These are the qualities that define man as man. These are the reasons for my becoming a counselor-psychotherapist rather than a veterinarian or animal trainer.

A Psychology of Human Development and Behavior

A personal cosmology and a conception of man provide the philosophical undergirding for a psychotherapy. The next challenge is to supplement the philosophic conceptions of man's origin, existence, and essence with a theoretical comprehension of human development and behavior. Assuming the other physical and biological phenomena descriptive of human growth and development, the formulations here are restricted, and appropriately so, to a) a theory of the structure and development of the healthy personality, b) the nature of disordered or disruptive behavior, and c) a theory of therapy or behavior modification.

A Theory of Personality

A four-dimensional format is utilized to facilitate the systematic integration of concepts and constructs derived from a variety of theoretical sources. An integrative theory of personality will be developed around: a definition, the structure, the dynamics, and the development of personality, respectively.

A Definition

Our English word *personality* stems from the Latin *persona*, which referred initially to the mask worn by theatrical players in ancient Roman drama. In time the concept took on three basic meanings: the *outward appearance* of the player, the *role* the player assumed in the drama, and the actual *self* of the player. In like fashion, personality has been understood typically as the outward appearance of an individual as perceived by others, and the true being of the individual (English & English, 1958). In the most elementary sense, personality is a behavior pattern consisting essentially of what an individual is intrinsically and what he does overtly in an existential moment of his life.

A formal definition is offered with appreciation to Brussel and Cantzlaar (1967) for their contribution. *Personality is the totality of the behavioral and attitudinal characteristics by which one is recognized by self and others as a unique individual. This holistic pattern is a mosaic of both visible and invisible factors, of conscious learning experiences and unconscious processes, of intrinsic and acquired qualities, features and attributes. The mosaic is ever changing as the individual, the PERSON, actualizes himself in his world. Thus, personality is the person expressing himself holistically and uniquely in existential situations.*

Having written a definition, we hasten to endorse Thorne's

(1967) position that "the term *personality* is only a high level semantic abstraction or descriptive generalization attempting to characterize the individuality of a *person* — the conscious Being, the individual running the business of life in the world" [pp. 1, 2, 21].

An explanatory word is needed with regard to the use of the expression "healthy personality" in this volume. The term "healthy" is *not* used in a medical sense to suggest the possibility of an "abnormal," "diseased," or "sick" personality; rather, the concept is used synonymously with Maslow's (1954) "self-actualizing person," Roger's (1961) "fully functioning person," and Landsman's (1968) "beautiful and noble person."

The Structure of Personality

The person is a holistic organism but he is not monolithic. The person is fundamentally a complex integration of physical (somatic) and non-physical (psychic, rational, and spiritual) dimensions and attributes. In the functioning organism, the two domains are indivisible and nondualistic. Though the physical and nonphysical aspects of personality are organismically bonded, we postulate that the psychic, rational, and spiritual dimensions are to be distinguished from the body *per se;* and, that they, collectively, comprise the true inner being — not to be understood as a homunculus — which is manifested holistically through the medium of the body. And just as the somatic and nonsomatic aspects are united but distinguishable, so are the psychic, rational, and spiritual dimensions of personality.

We concur with Rychlak (1973) that one of the questions to be answered in personality theory is: "What is the essential structure of personality? Or, if structure is to be disregarded, what are we to substitute" (p. 20)? An effort is made here to provide an outline of a structural framework for comprehending personality.

THE PHYSICAL PERSON: The starting point in seeking a structure of personality is with the most obvious and absolutely essential element, the *primus locus* of personhood, the body — without the body, there is no person. Allport (1955) has well observed that the first aspect an individual encounters is the bodily me. To a young child his body is he. The Gestaltists present a valid point: "I don't have a body, I *am* my body" (Perls, 1969). The physical senses, sensorimotor activities, internal sensations, and the body image combine to form the basis for conceiving oneself as a person. Simply stated, the body is the bio-psycho-spiritual space in which and the sensorimotor vehicle by which the individual builds and actualizes himself.

THE FEELING PERSON: Indistinguishable from bodily sensations are those psychological phenomena which can be labeled quite appropriately as *the feeling person*. These phenomena — feelings, emotions, desires, sentiments, affections, etc. — constitute the less rational part of the individual. In Freudian thought, the Id, characterized by instinctual impulsiveness and the primary process, represents grossly the affective dimension of personality. The feeling person can be equated with the psychological or ego state of the Child in Transactional Analysis, where the Child is the "felt concept of life" (Berne, 1972; Harris, 1969). Too, the feeling person is synonymous with Roger's (1961) concept of the sensory and visceral "experiencing organism." This sentient element in the personality runs the gamut of human emotions and experiences.

The emotional aspect of the personal psyche (soul-life) is, in many ways, suggestive of "passive reasoning." But perhaps we would do well not to go beyond calling it the "wisdom of the organism" or "gut sense."

THE THINKING PERSON: A striking feature of the human being is the capacity for creative reasoning and rational thinking. This phenomenon in personality can be described best as "active mind" or "intelligence." The Greeks used the term *nous* to describe this rational and intelligent principle in man. The more rational and reflective parts of the *psyche* also contribute to *the thinking person*. A primary connotation of *psyche* is the *mind*. We also want to incorporate the second major connotation, namely *psyche* as a *rational soul*. The thinking person approximates a) Freud's concept of "Ego" or "reality principle" based on the secondary process, b) Ellis' "rational thinker," and c) Berne and Harris' "Adult" ego state which refers to the "thought concept of life" and is marked by intentionality and finding rational solutions to life's problems.

THE VALUING PERSON: The individual's values and attitudes comprise another dimension of his personality. It appears to make little difference whether we call this a "system of moral and ethical values" or use the more sophisticated term "conscience." Our *valuing person* reflects, among other theoretical constructs, a) the culture-based "Superego" posited by psychoanalytic and dynamic approaches to personality, b) the "responsible individual" who lives according to a satisfactory standard of behavior — a concept of "right and wrong" — as presented in Glasser's (1965) Reality Therapy, and c) the Transactional Analysis construct of "Parent" used to depict the "taught or acquired concept of life." In addition to the assumption that the conscience consists essentially of learned attitudes and values, we submit that the individual possesses an innate sense of morality. Both the Greek and Latin roots, *suneidesis* and *conscientia,* respectively, are composite words meaning *co-knowledge* ("with" or "together" plus "knowledge") which suggest an agreement between learned values and one's inner moral beingness. Thus, an intrinsic moral awareness combines with learned values to produce the valuing person.

THE DECISIVE PERSON: In addition to feeling, thinking, and valuing, the individual can act decisively. Some have called this "volition," others refer to it as "conation." The writer prefers the Greek concept of *boulema* which denotes a deliberately chosen design and purpose and the *power to execute or actualize* that which is purposed or intended. Existentialists (e.g., May, 1969; Frankl, 1969) make reference to this same dimension of personality when they claim man (the individual) is free and has the power or will to commit himself to a course of action. Similarly, the Gestalt view (Perls, 1969) sees in man the capacity to transcend from environmental support and stand as a self-supporting and self-regulating organism in his world. In essence, the person has the intrinsic power to be self-determining and self-actualizing. Whatever this "power" is — volition, conation, *boulema,* freedom, will, commitment — it includes emotions, intellect, and values *but* it is much more than these.

THE SPIRITUAL PERSON: There is in the individual an element inextricably related to the *psyche* (mind-soul) and the *nous* (reason-intelligence) but distinct from them. The Greeks called this component of personality the *pneuma* and the Latins conceived it as the *spiritus.* Historically, the *spirit* has been understood, particularly by those influenced by the Hebraic-Christian world view, to be the *vital principle* and the *seat of conscious functions* in man. This is the characteristically positive dimension of personality and is concerned with altruism, justice, love, truth, beauty, benevolence, meaning, relationships, and immortality. The spiritual person is central in Frankl's (1962, 1965, 1969) Logotherapy. It is this dimension in man that bridges the physical and metaphysical domains of human existence.

THE SELF-CONSCIOUS PERSON: The integral of the preceding dimensions of personality represents the individuality of the person. The unique integration of his bodily sense and concomitant phenomena, his feelings, thoughts, his values, his decisions-commitments, and his spiritual realities leads the individual in time to the phenomenal-existential status of *This is I.* The individual is *aware* or *self-conscious* of his *personhood* or *selfhood* — he knows who he is, he has an *identity.* (Later, when we discuss the development of personality, the concepts "Self" and "Identity" will be placed in clearer focus.)

The Dynamics of Personality

The behavior of an individual does not originate from a vacuum. Human behavior is intentional and purposive or teleological. Thus, there are incentives which prompt behavior toward specific goals or objectives. The dynamics which operate in the person to produce behavior patterns, indeed, "mold" a particular personality style, have been identified with a variety of concepts. Frequently used terms are instinct, drive, need, stimulus, cue, impulse, and motive. But are all these constructs necessary to account for behavior?

It is our position that the "needs-motivation" construct is sufficient to define the dynamics of human behavior and personality — needs of the human organism motivate behavior. The model fits best the Gestalt point of view. The individual (or organism) exists inseparably with his environment, though distinct from it. The relationships and interactions between the individual and the environment form his phenomenal world. In a given period of time a particular need dominates the field and emerges as the *figure* while everything else in the phenomenal world becomes the *ground.*

> The phenomenal world is organized by the needs of the individual. *Needs energize behavior and organize it* on the subjective-perceptual level and on the objective-motor level. The individual [perceives a need or needs and] then carries out the necessary [motoric] activities in order to satisfy the needs. After satisfaction . . . the concern with the particular figure [the need and accompanying factors] disappears or recedes into the background, and something new emerges. We have *a hierarchy of needs continually developing, organizing the figures of experience, and disappearing.* We describe this process . . . as progressive formation and destruction of perceptual and motor gestalts. [Wallen, 1971, p. 9; emphasis added]

Viewing the person from the motivational perspective, life is a process of forming and destructing gestalts — moving from one fulfilled need to another. And in the case of the integrated individual, he is "a person in whom this process is going on constantly without interruption. New figures are continually being formed. *When the needs are satisfied, these figures are destroyed and replaced by others, permitting the needs next highest in the dominance hierarchy to organize behavior* and perceptual experience" (*Ibid.,* p. 10; emphasis added). In satisfying his needs, the individual is motivated as a whole organism rather than a part.

Adopting Maslow's (1954, 1967) hierarchical arrangement as a workable schema, a catalog is provided below of the needs that motivate human behavior.

THE PERSON IS MOTIVATED BY PHYSIOLOGICAL NEEDS: The individual needs food, drink, warmth, rest, and sleep in order to maintain bodily homeostasis and to avoid the pain of hunger, thirst, frozenness, fatigue, and sleepiness. Among other physiological needs are the sexual desire and physical exercise. The human being is motivated both *to survive and to be free of pain, tension,* and/or *discomfort.* We can call this multi-motive either the "pleasure principle" (Freud) or the "enhancement of the organism" (Rogers). Until the individual "feels good" physiologically, he is unable to attend effectively to other needs — to grow and to actualize himself.

THE PERSON IS MOTIVATED BY SAFETY NEEDS: Not far removed from the physiological motivators of behavior are the needs for safety and security. The individual requires and seeks an orderly and trusted world which can provide him with a sense of social, economic, physical, psychological, and spiritual well-being. Any variable in the individual's world that poses as a threat or danger to his security becomes figural and all else background. Authentic progress is thwarted until this gestalt is completed and/or destructed.

THE PERSON IS MOTIVATED BY LOVE NEEDS: "The deepest need of man, says Fromm (1963), is *to overcome* his *separateness,* to leave the prison of his aloneness, his disunited existence . . . to reach out, unite himself in some form or another with man . . . *to achieve union*" (pp. 7, 8). Man has a need for relatedness, the need to belong, the need to share — give and receive — mature love (Fromm, 1955, 1963). Indeed, a basic psychological need of man is to love and be loved (Glasser, 1965). There are reasons enough to believe that "love is the principal developer of one's capacities for being human . . . and the only thing on earth that can produce the sense of belongingness and relatedness to the world of humanity" (Montagu, 1970, p. 467). The degree to which the individual's love needs are satisfied affects behavior and personality as much, if not more, than any other motivating factor.

THE PERSON IS MOTIVATED BY ESTEEM NEEDS: Another basic psychological need of the individual is *to feel worthwhile to self and to others* (Glasser, 1965). In order to have the feelings of self-confidence, worth, strength, capability, and adequacy, there must be first the satisfaction of the self-esteem/self-respect/self-regard needs (Rogers, 1959). The words of a popular song ask: "How can I be right for somebody else if I'm not right for me?" The need to feel right about self is a terribly strong motivating force in behavior and personality. If these needs are thwarted, the life style can become quite distorted to say the least.

THE PERSON IS MOTIVATED BY THE NEED TO ACTUALIZE HIMSELF: Again, excerpts from three contemporary songs express another need of the individual: "Do it or die, I've gotta try, I've gotta be me"; "You've got to make your own kind of music, sing your own special song"; and "I did it my way." The individual must stand in his world and actualize his potential in order to achieve the desire for self-fulfillment. *"What a man CAN be, he MUST be* or *he must become everything that he is capable of becoming"* (Maslow, 1954, pp. 91–92; emphasis added). The in vogue expressions "I want to do my own thing" and "That's my bag" are more than mere slang — they communicate at the gut level the desire to affirm oneself as a unique human being, vocationally or otherwise.

THE PERSON IS MOTIVATED BY COGNITIVE NEEDS: Man, as a rational and intelligent being, is motivated by the *desire to know, to explore* and *explain* the unknown, *to satisfy* his *curiosity* about the mysterious, *to discover* new truth through experimentation, *to give system and order* to chaos, and *to master and understand* bodies of truth. When the more basic human needs have been satisfied and the individual is unable to fulfill his cognitive needs, he becomes bored, intellectually inanimate, and frustrated. The behavior patterns and the personality style characteristic of a given individual reflect in a definite measure the manner in which and the degree to which he gratifies his cognitive needs.

THE PERSON IS MOTIVATED BY PHILOSOPHIC-SPIRITUAL NEEDS: The individual, a spiritual being, *seeks to find meaning* to life and existence. This striving to find a meaning in one's life is the primary motivational force in man; a philosophy of life, a set of values that pull him, ideals and values that he is able to live and even to die for (Frankl, 1962). The individual human being needs a frame of orientation and devotion — a means of making sense of the many puzzling phenomena surrounding him (Fromm, 1955). He desires, in some individualized form, a comprehensive philosophic-religious outlook that serves as a unifying approach to life and existence.

> Quandaries, predicaments, cross-purposes, guilt, and ultimate mysteries are handled under this comprehensive commitment. This commitment is partially intellectual, but more fundamentally motivational. It is integral, covering everything in experience and everything beyond experience; it makes room for scientific fact and emotional fact. It is *a hunger for, and a commitment to, an ideal unification of one's life,* but always under a unifying conception of the nature of all existence. [Allport, 1968, p. 151; emphasis added]

The individual has just as great a need and hunger for a philosophy of life as he does for vitamins and minerals; and the person without a system of values or without a philosophy of life is in an unhealthy psychological state (Maslow, 1971).

THE PERSON IS MOTIVATED BY AESTHETIC NEEDS: Man has both the capacity and the desire to experience "the true, the good, and the beautiful." The individual defines himself in part by the nature of his pursuing and satisfying the *needs for beauty, design, harmony, symmetry, closure, order, creativity,* and *orchestration.* Individual taste regarding matters such as food, clothing, housing, art and music, geographic landscape, and the use of leisure suggest specific motivators of behavior and personality. The creative and artistic individual, regardless of profession or status, is a person actualizing himself as he fulfills both cognitive and aesthetic needs.

Comments

The preceding *catalogue raisonne* is designed to be representative of the basic determinants of human behavior and personality. These motivating needs, though arranged in a hierarchy, are not to be considered as fixed nor as mutually exclusive. They should be construed as the relative order in which the human being seeks personal gratification. Aspects of several differential needs may combine in an existential situation to become figural. For instance, the preparation of this manuscript is now the figure in my phenomenal world and involves at least the esteem, self-actualization, and cognitive needs. Nor does the individual necessarily have to be fully aware of all the motivational dynamics in a given situation — there is room for both the conscious and the unconscious motivation. Whatever might be the nature of the need, however, the entire individual (organism) is motivated and functions holistically to satisfy that need.

The Development of Personality

The human infant possesses at birth, barring incapacitating biological or organic defect, the potential to become a self-actualizing individual. The kind of person the infant eventually will become depends largely upon his postnatal experiences. In this section we will be concerned with the variables involved in the process of building a personal identity — or acquiring individuality as a unique person. Attention will be focused, first, on the phenomenal matrix that produces the self and, then, on the process of individuation.

The Experiencing Person in a Phenomenal Universe*

From the moment of birth the developing human being is an experiencing person located, relative to himself, at the center of a universe of physical, social, and spiritual phenomena. The experiencing occurs at the "contact boundary" between the human organism and the universe or environment. As articulated earlier, the human organism is distinct but not separated from the universe. The individual experiences or makes contact with the universe through both sensory awareness and motor behavior. The interactions and relationships between the person and the universe can be considered as the "person/universe field." As the human organism contacts and interacts with the universe, a world of experience or learning develops which is private to the individual. This private world of experience may be viewed as the "phenomenal field." The experiencing person, his phenomenal field, and the universe of phenomena are illustrated in Figure 3.

FIGURE 3

The Experiencing Person in the Phenomenal Universe

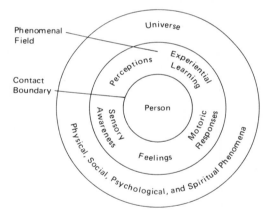

In the early years, experiential learning is "recorded" primarily at the feeling level with relatively little "conscious" experiencing. Thus, most of the young individual's experiences or learning form the ground, and he the figure, of the phenomenal field. But elements of prior experiences can emerge and become part of the figure when an organismic need must be satisfied, and then recede

* The author wishes to acknowledge his indebtedness to Kurt Lewin, Carl Rogers, Frederick Perls, Ralph Hefferline, and Paul Goodman for their influence and contributions.

back into ground. For example, the infant discovers that his crying gets the attention of his parents or caretakers; therefore, whenever he feels the hunger sensation, the "learned and forgotten" cause and effect association between crying and receiving food emerges from the ground and becomes a figural component in meeting the immediate need. When the hunger is satiated, the "meaning" of crying again becomes oblivious ground.

The phenomenal field is continually changing and expanding. Each new contact with the universe adds another element — be it conscious or unconscious learning — to the individual's private world. Simultaneously, the individual extends himself a bit farther into the universe *and* incorporates parts of the universe into himself. As the infant continues to interact with or experience his universe — physical and social — he gradually forms concepts, attitudes, and feelings about himself, about the universe, and about his relationships with the universe, particularly those relationships with people. The individual learns to perceive the world (realm of objective-external reality) and himself (realm of objective-internal reality) in terms of how the world treats him, especially as experienced via parental care. These perceptions constitute "subjective-normative reality" for the individual. Sometime during the first three years of life, a portion of the total phenomenal field is recognized as the unique possession of the individual. The child knows what and who belong to him, he can recognize himself in the mirror and in photographs, senses that his name has significance, and knows his likes and dislikes. This differentiated portion of the phenomenal field composes the "Self" of the individual. This is the "I," "me," "my," "mine," or "myself" and includes the fused perceptions and evaluations of both that which is intrinsic to the individual and that which is external to him. Figure 4 contains a schematization of the "Self" (to be discussed more fully in the next section).

The Emerging Concept of Self*

The fact that the phenomenal world of the individual is ever changing means, necessarily, that the "Self" is also dynamic. The first awareness of one's separate existence as an "I" is the mere beginning of a life-long process of building, discovering, and becoming individual personhood. Certainly, at some point in the de-

---

* Among the many individuals whose ideas are reflected here, the following ones are the principals: Alfred Adler, Eric Berne, John Dollard, Neal Miller, Erik Erikson, William Glasser, Thomas Harris, Robert Havighurst, Karen Horney, Carl Rogers, and Harry S. Sullivan.

FIGURE 4

The Self of the Experiencing Person

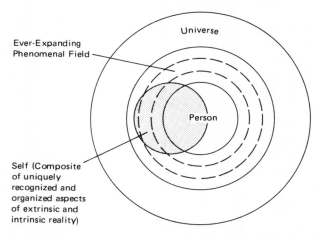

velopmental process the individual achieves a rather stable view of himself — but when and how?

The human being is a living and learning and, therefore, a growing organism. And "anything that grows has a ground plan, and out of this ground plan the parts arise, each part having its time of special ascendancy, until all parts have arisen to form a functioning whole" (Erikson, 1959, p. 52). The preceding statement represents the "epigenetic principle" on which Erikson has erected a theory of personality growth and development. A number of basic assumptions underlie the theory: 1) the life cycle consists of eight psychosocial stages of personality growth in which the individual must establish new basic orientations to himself and his social world; 2) personality development continues throughout the whole of life; 3) each stage or phase of the life cycle is characterized by a specific bipolar developmental task to be accomplished; 4) each of the eight components is systematically related to all others and they all depend mutually on the successful development in the proper sequence of each component; and 5) each component exists in some elemental form before its decisive and critical time normally arrives.

We reiterate that a primary motivation in human behavior is the desire to maintain, enhance, and actualize the experiencing organism. It is further assumed here that the phenomenal field and learning theory are indivisible factors in the growth of personality. With these premises in mind, we shall proceed to build an integrative conception of personality development around Erikson's epigenetic theory.

INFANCY: The infant's first major psychological learning concerns his trust of the universe, other people, and himself. Granted, the concepts the infant holds are essentially nonverbal, yet they serve as guiding principles for his valuing process. Sometime during the first year of life the young individual judges either that "the world is safe, can be trusted, and that I'm a *good me*," or that "the world is unsafe, cannot be trusted, and I'm a *bad me*." The infant's decision is based on whether the parents/caretakers are loving, comforting, and helpful, or rejecting, anxious, and hurtful to him. The quality of the social interaction in this phase leaves a lasting mark on the personality — the person. If *basic trust* becomes the reality, then a secure and socially courageous self is in the making. But on the other hand, if *basic mistrust* is the experience, an insecure and withdrawing person is most likely to emerge.

EARLY CHILDHOOD: During the second and third years of life, there are a) pronounced development in verbal skills, b) increased motor behavior, and c) difficulties in learning to feed oneself and to control elimination. The child wants to be proud of himself and seeks to be autonomous. He needs very much the approval of significant persons. If parents provide the proper amount of freedom and are generous with positive reinforcement, the child will achieve a *sense of autonomy* and a feeling of *I'M OK*. If parents are pushy, overprotective, overpermissive, critical, and/or punitive, the child will *doubt himself* and have *feelings of shame* and *I'M NOT OK*. Much of the learning in this phase is also at the feeling level due to the lack of symbols adequate to give experiences cognitive existence. The young person who departs this stage with unmet needs — with a sense of shame and doubt along with a core of negative dynamics functioning at the sub-awareness state — is well on his way to building a handicapped personality.

MIDDLE CHILDHOOD: The child of four or five has substantial control over his body, possesses a fair command of language, and exhibits a vivid imagination and rich fantasy life. The child is interested in knowing what kind of person he is going to be. Although he identifies with the parents, and fantasizes being like them, the child has a strong desire to follow his own initiative. Learning to distinguish right and wrong, or developing a conscience, is a concern of the four or five year old. The inquisitive mind of the child at this stage is filled with questions. If parents provide freedom and opportunity for self-initiated play and motor behavior, respect the child's questions and answer them openly and honestly, and do not deride or inhibit fantasy and motor behaviors, then they reinforce the *initiative* of the child. But if the contrary is true of parental behavior, then the child will acquire a sense of *guilt* and *intensified NOT OKness.*

By this time in his development, the individual has laid down a "life plan" or "life script" which frames the meaning of existence and shapes his goals. If he has achieved a basic trust toward life, feels autonomous, and possesses self-initiative, the child senses a basic OKness and comes at life in a creative and socially effective style. But, the child who has a basic mistrust toward life, and feels ashamed, guilty, stupid, and no good, could be already living a "life lie" which is based on a fictional goal and manifests itself in neurotic manipulation. Either way, OK or NOT OK, *the child is living out, consciously and unconsciously, a learned concept of self — a style of life.*

LATE CHILDHOOD: During the "juvenile" or elementary school years, age period from 6 to 12, the child is capable of deductive reasoning and occupies himself with a) learning the skills necessary for social and competitive games, b) learning to cooperate and to play according to rules, c) learning an appropriate social role as a sexual being, d) developing basic skills in reading, writing, and calculating, e) developing a set of ethical and moral values, and f) achieving personal independence. The child wants to feel useful and needs to have a sense that he can design and build things well. It is important to him how parents, teachers, and peers view his performance. If the child receives praise and encouragement in his efforts to be creative and industrious, he develops a *sense of adequacy and competency.* On the other hand, if the child is chided in his attempts at physical, social, and educational achievement, he develops a *sense of inadequacy and inferiority.* Thus, at the conclusion of this phase of growth in personality, either an enhancing quality or a crippling attitude is added to the evolving image of self.

ADOLESCENCE: Adolescence, roughly the ages 13–18, is a period of growth marked by physiological, psychological, and social revolution. Rapid body growth, physical sexual maturity, increased mental capacity, and a multitude of new feelings, sensations, and desires combine concurrently to create psychological turbulence in the teenage person. It seems to the adolescent that past learning, prior experiences, and former relationships have lost their relevance — there is no sense of continuity.

As he stands on the threshold of adulthood, the adolescent must struggle with a sizeable number of concerns. There is the constant struggle to accept the rapidly changing physique. The body image is so important, it seems, to one's sense of sexual adequacy and social desirability. Achieving a satisfying social role as a sexual being — masculine or feminine — does not always come easily. Moving from chumships with same sexed persons to intimacy with those of the opposite sex can be difficult; indeed, it can bring painful loneliness. Establishing emotional independence of parents and other significant adults can be disconcerting at times. Then, there is the matter of preparing for a career in order to achieve assurance of economic independence. The adolescent must also develop intellectual and social skills and behaviors sufficient for civic competence. Another chief task is the acquisition of a system of moral and ethical values as a guide for behavior.

Essential to success in this stage of personality development is a *sense of psychosocial identity — "a persistent sameness within oneself and a persistent sharing of some kind of essential character with others"* (Erikson, 1959, p. 102; emphasis added). This is the time to form a *stable sense of self.* To achieve such an identity or sense of self, there must first be a vital sense of trust, autonomy, initiative, adequacy, and OKness. This means an integration of all previous learning, experiences, images, and identifications into a working, harmonious, and meaningful whole. The individual knows who he is and possesses a realistic philosophy of life. Such a person has a *success identity* and can actualize himself in his phenomenal world.

On the other hand, the young person who reaches adolescence with a sense of mistrust, shame, doubt, inadequacy, guilt, inferiority, and NOT OKness suffers identity confusion. He does not know who he really is, nor where or to whom he belongs, and lacks a workable philosophy of life. This person has a *failure identity* and is unable to actualize himself; therefore, he lives a "life lie" in "search for glory."

YOUNG ADULTHOOD: The period 19–30 in the life cycle is highly characterized by social relationships such as courtship and marriage, marital adjustment, child rearing, engagement in productive work, assuming civic responsibilities, and seeking membership in social groups.

A basic desire or need of the young adult is *intimacy* with the spouse and friends of both sexes. The need to share *mature love* with other persons — to enjoy reciprocity in social-personal *union.* But it is only after a sense of personal identity has been attained that real intimacy with either spouse or friend is possible. Thus, only the individual who emerges from adolescence with a solid psychosocial identity has the capacity for true friendship, mature love, and authentic intimacy — the capacity to be a self-actualizing and truly productive person.

The young adult without a wholesome sense of self will tend toward *isolation*. His social relationships will be marked by one of three basic movements in life: 1) *movement toward people* in order to secure love and affection — usually, some form of symbiosis without authentic union; 2) *movement away from people* in order to achieve independence; or 3) *movement against people* in order to attain power, prestige, possession, and mastery. The isolated person is essentially egocentric, manipulative, and possessive.

MIDDLE AGE: Middle age, roughly the age of 30–60, can be either the most rewarding or the most disappointing stage in the individual's life. The middle age adult typically is concerned with a) achieving a *sense of generativity* as a responsible civic and social being, b) being an effective parent, c) experiencing fulfillment in creative and productive work, d) providing well for the needs of the family, e) fostering a meaningful relationship with the spouse, f) enjoying creative leisure, and g) adjusting to physiological changes unique to middle age.

If middle age was prefaced by a solid psychosocial identity and the attainment of personal intimacy, then the individual stands the good chance of becoming a self-actualizing and altruistic person. The higher needs — cognitive, philosophic, and aesthetic — will be satisfied through various forms of altruistic concern and creativity.

But the individual who has failed to form a wholesome sense of self and lacks the capacity for intimacy, is likely to fall into a state of *self-absorption* in which the gratification of personal needs becomes the predominant concern. Rather than self-actualization, the person experiences *stagnation* and *boredom* in an existential vacuum. The self-absorbed person employs a variety of means to compensate for his deficiencies and to resolve his frustrations and need for intimacy — e.g., use of alcohol and drugs, increased sexual experiences involving several sex partners, increased membership in clubs and social groups with little real involvement in any, spending more time on the job, securing bigger and better material possessions, and suicide.

LATE ADULTHOOD: The individual of age 60 or older must give attention to matters such as decreasing physical strength and health, retirement and diminished income, incapacitation or death of the spouse, sustaining affiliation with a circle of confidants, and maintaining a sense of social significance.

The older adult realizes that his major efforts or contributions are nearing completion. Such awareness will provoke either a *sense of integrity* or a *sense of despair*. If the individual can review his life with a deep sense of satisfaction, believing that he has fulfilled his plans and intentions, and is able to discern meaningful continuity between the phases of his existence, then a sense of worth, significance, usefulness, and success is experienced. But if the individual considers his life as a series of failures, disappointments, missed opportunities, wrong decisions, and is unable to integrate meaningfully his past experiences, the present situation, and future possibilities, then he tends to resign from life to await remorsefully the certainty of death.

Summary

Thus, the growth and development of the physical, feeling, thinking, valuing, deciding, spiritual, and self-conscious person is a from-the-womb-to-the-tomb process. The individuality of the person emerges from and is manifested in an ever changing phenomenal field of experiential learning. The individual forms a preconscious life plan or script during his first five years of existence and this prototype persists to some degree throughout life. The life plan is modified either for better or worse as the individual faces phase-specific crises in the developmental process. The experiences, values, images, and identifications of the first twelve years of life either culminate in a wholesome psychosocial identity or produce identity confusion during adolescence. This psychosocial identity, or the lack of an identity, forms the basis for coming at life as an adult. The healthy personality stems from the sequential satisfaction of basic human needs and is characterized by a vital sense of truth, autonomy, initiative, industry, identity, intimacy, generativity, integrity, success, and OKness.

The Nature of Problematic Behavior

Up to this point the major concern has been the development of the self-actualizing person. We have used the concept "healthy personality" as being representative of the self-actualizing person, with the realization that the metaphor of health is an undesirable one to some counselor-psychotherapists (e.g., Robert White, 1973). The very existence of a profession called "psychotherapy" (healing, restoring, making whole, or strengthening the mind, soul, or life) suggests rather strongly that something is wrong with the human situation. The task at hand is to provide a workable theory of behavior disturbance or disquietude. Specifically, an adequate answer must be given to the question: Why does an individual need or seek counseling and psychotherapy?

Abnormality and the Myth of Mental Illness

When the term "healthy personality" is used as a general description of the phenomenal-personal-social-psychological-existential state of a particular individual or group of individuals, the dialectician immediately thinks with opposites and concludes that a "sick personality" is implied for another group of individuals. Such dichotomous reasoning is unwarranted.

The position taken here regarding the concepts of "abnormality" and/or "mental illness" parallels the thinking of Szasz (1960, 1961, 1974) and Ullmann and Krasner (1969). It has been the custom for a number of centuries to define abnormality and mental illness either as disorders in thinking and behavior due to some neurological defect or as deformities of personality. Regardless of which view is espoused, an abnormality or mental illness represents a deviance from specific psychosocial, ethical, and legal norms. Granted, human beings do incur serious problems in living but "behaviors traditionally called abnormal [or mental illness] are no different, either quantitatively or qualitatively, in their development and maintenance from other learned behaviors" [Ullmann & Krasner, p. 1]. Unless a biological or organic defect can be detected in the human organism, there is wisdom in assuming that

> . . . mental illnesses do not exist . . . The notion of mental illness has outlived whatever usefulness it might have had and now functions merely as a convenient myth . . . the phenomena now called mental illnesses [should] be removed from the category of illnesses, and be regarded as the expressions of man's struggle with the problem of how he should live. [Szasz, 1960]

While abnormal behavior and mental illness are at best convenient labels used by an observer to define social and behavioral phenomena, the social-psychological occurrences to which the labels refer do exist in reality. But, rather than being abnormal *per se*, the observed behavior is the reasonable outcome of the person's total history of experiential learning in his unique phenomenal world. Many human behaviors are clear-cut deviations from cultural norms, but it is the circumspect counselor-psychotherapist who studies diligently both the person and his situation *and* avoids the labels abnormal and mentally ill. It is best to regard all behavior as the meaningful attempt of the human organism to adjust to itself and to its environment* than to categorize some behaviors as abnormal, or as constituting disease entities (Rogers, 1951).

---

* Sometimes we find it hard to believe that behaviors such as ruthless, brutal, and bizarre murder and torture are meaningful attempts toward adjustment to life. Yet, when we examine the social-psychological history of the exhibitor, the behavior pattern then "makes sense."

Frustrated Satisfaction of Basic Needs

The problems in living which are presented to the professional therapist can be traced in the larger part to unmet needs of the human organism. In the discussions under the headings "Dynamics" and "Development" of personality, reference was made to the negative effects which ungratified basic needs and failure to achieve success with sequential developmental tasks have on the psychological well-being of the individual. Most of the individuals who seek counseling and psychotherapy have not reached self-actualizing status nor do they possess a wholesome psychosocial identity. They are unable to actualize, maintain, and enhance their existence in a realistic, mature, and self-fulfilling manner. Consequently, in order to maintain whatever sense of self that does exist, they resort to neurotic behaviors of various levels of intensity. Although they can function in their world, these individuals feel, to some degree, that they are inadequate, ineffective, no good, unloved, unwanted, insecure, unstable, and/or inferior. They are quite miserable in their existence and life seems to have little meaning. It is virtually impossible for these persons to establish and sustain mature interpersonal relationships due to the intrapersonal incongruence so characteristic of individuals whose satisfaction of basic needs has been frustrated.

In some individuals the deprivation is of such magnitude, in both the gratification of needs and success with developmental tasks or crises, that private worlds are created which have little or no correspondence with external reality. For lack of a better word, these individuals are the so-called "psychotics" who are out of touch with self, other people, their environment, and life.

Inappropriate Learning

Inappropriate learning constitutes a second major source of problems in living. In this volume learning is considered inappropriate if it is either insufficient in amount, inaccurate in content, improperly timed, or experienced under undesirable conditions. Thus, inappropriate learning is necessarily a concomitant of unmet human needs. Consequently, the troubles we deal with professionally as counselor-psychotherapists lie in the realm of learned behavior and have arisen from unfortunate conditionings, undesirable patterns of reinforcement, defensive inhibitions, and poorly devised or worn-out strategies of adaptation (White, 1973). Clients manifest these troubles in the forms of deficient decision-making skills, ineffective academic and vocational skills, inappropriate social and civic skills, and self-defeating fears, doubts, guilt, shame, and anxieties.

Existential Crises

Other problems in living arise from what might be called "existential crises." Events such as the death of a close relative or beloved friend, the loss of some prized material possession or one's job, being betrayed/abandoned by a confidant or lover, failure to realize the fulfillment of personal plans, and being confronted with a terminal disease or a disfiguring bodily injury can bring psychological disquiet, even to the most self-actualizing person. The disturbance — despodency, depression, remorse, etc. — can be either acute or chronic depending on the emotional-mental resilience and intrapersonal integration of the particular individual. In such crises, the individual needs and seeks support and nurturance, if nothing more.

Summary

Except in cases which involve organic lesions and/or biogenetic malfunction, clients suffer from neither abnormality nor mental illness. The problems human beings incur in living arise from unmet needs, inappropriate learning, and existential crises. All behavior is best construed as the meaningful attempts of the organism to maintain, actualize, and enhance itself in its environment. When these attempts become frustrated and the individual feels ineffective in adjusting to self and his world, he seeks professional help.

The Nature of Psychotherapy

If all behavior can be viewed as attempts of the person to adjust to self and environment, then psychotherapy, from the standpoint of the client, is but another effort toward maintaining, enhancing, and actualizing the organism. And from the standpoint of the counselor-therapist, psychotherapy is an introgression into the life-space of the client-person to assist him with a) the fulfilling of unmet needs, b) the learning of new skills and attitudes sufficient for effective and enjoyable living, and/or c) the resolution of existential crises. Perceptually, the client perceives the counselor-therapist as being in possession of the personal attributes and the professional skills adequate to help him with his concerns; the counselor-therapist perceives the client as a worthy human being, and perceives himself as competent to facilitate the behavior change desired by the client. Essentially, psychotherapy is a personal-social-phenomenal-psychological-existential relationship between one person (the client — or a group of clients) who is experiencing a problem in living and another person (the counselor-therapist) who is personally and professionally prepared to effect therapeutic gain in behavior and personality.

Motives for Entering Psychotherapy

Rychlak (1973) has observed that both the client and the counselor-psychotherapist enter the counseling relationship with one of three general motives: the *scholarly,* the *ethical,* and the *curative.*

The *scholarly motive* has reference to a) the client who wishes to engage an in-depth study of self, to find out about himself, to gain insight into his behavior and personality; and b) the counselor-psychotherapist whose primary concerns are to understand the dynamics of human behavior, to teach the client something about himself, and to provide insight into the cause(s) of his problem.

The *ethical motive* is more concerned with values, meaning, re-lationships, and growth. The client desires a relationship with a professional person who is caring and accepting and who can help him to grow toward self-realization. The client wants a non-threatening environment in which he can examine himself in his own terms. The counselor-psychotherapist seeks to encounter the client as an equal human being in a supportive and therapeutic interpersonal relationship. The major concern of the therapist is the fostering of self-acceptance, self-esteem, self-worth, self-growth, self-determination, and self-actualization in the client.

The *curative motive* is descriptive of the client who conceives himself as abnormal, comes to therapy to get well, play the "sick patient" role, and expects to be the passive recipient of magical clinical help. The curative-minded therapist focuses primarily on symptom removal and seeks to heal the patient in the shortest period of time possible by manipulating both the client and the environment. Therapeutic cure is assessed on the basis of the ab-sence of symptomatic behavior.

We would assume that neither the client nor the therapist has a consistently singular or exclusive motive for engaging in psychotherapy. Rather, various combinations of the motives are characteristic of both client and psychotherapist at different stages of the therapy process. In integrative counseling and psychotherapy the ethical motive is primary, with the scholarly motive in a secondary but indispensable position, while the cura-tive motive is of minor significance.

Forms of Psychotherapy

Closely paralleling the three motives for counseling and psychotherapy are three basic forms or varieties of psychotherapy which have been identified by Wolberg (1954) as *reconstructive insight* therapy, *re-educative insight* therapy, and *supportive* therapy. Other writers have placed all psychotherapies under two classifications: *insight* therapy and *action* therapy. This writer prefers the "action" concept over the "supportive" label as the third therapeutic form in Wolberg's triad. The term "supportive" is somewhat descriptive of the facilitative nature of re-educative insight psychotherapy.

Reconstructive insight psychotherapy seeks to bring the individual to an awareness of his unconscious conflicts and their causes, which hinder interpersonal relationships and disrupt the modes of coping with and/or adjusting to self and the external world. Through the use of verbal techniques such as free association, interpretation, handling transference and resistance, life style analysis, and dream analysis, efforts are made a) to alter the basic structure of character or life script, b) to foster the development of a wholesome emotional-mental life with the creation of new adaptive potentialities which were thwarted in the course of the individual's psychosocial development, and c) to restore the individual to a state of effective living which is free of neurotic manipulation and defenses. Freudian psychoanalysis, analytical psychology, individual psychology, neo-Freudian approaches, and transactional analysis are representative of reconstructive insight psychotherapy.

Re-educative insight psychotherapy generally places a high premium on the relationship between the client and therapist as being both the vehicle that promotes therapeutic change and a model which can be followed by the client to establish interpersonal relationships outside the therapy encounter. The focus is on achieving insight into the more conscious aspects of personality and disturbing behavior. Only limited attention is given to the past, the analysis of transference, and the interpretation of dreams. Instead, techniques such as reflection, Socratic dialogue, confrontation, and psychodrama are used in the here-and-now existence to assist the client with a reorganization or clarification of his feelings, values, attitudes, and disruptive behavior patterns. The desired outcome is a congruent, self-regulating individual who a) can adjust meaningfully to his personal-phenomenal-social-psychological-spiritual world, b) is able to realize and actualize his personal strengths and potentialities, and c) lives and functions with minimal personal deficiencies and discomforts. Among the numerous re-educative insight psychotherapies, the following ones are illustrative examples: Gestalt therapy, reality therapy, client-centered psychotherapy, logotherapy, and rational-emotive psychotherapy.

Action psychotherapy is based on the assumption that all behavior, adaptive and maladaptive alike, is learned. Psychotherapy is actually nothing more than providing all the conditions necessary for new and appropriate learning. The focus is principally an overt behavior or symptoms with little interest in the "causes" of behavior, except the conditions which surrounded the learning of the maladaptive behavior. Social-learning principles are applied in the counseling-therapy process to eliminate undesired, ineffective, and defeating behaviors and to introduce new and more effective modes of behaving. The following are some of the methods used to overcome problems such as indecisiveness, poor academic performance, vocational maladjustment, inability to relate well interpersonally, and harassing fears and anxieties: assertive training, positive reinforcement, social modeling, systematic desensitization, behavior rehearsal, and contact desensitization. The client is *actively* involved in the therapy process which includes both the counseling interview and the practice of specified behaviors in the social milieu. Action psychotherapy is exemplified in behavior therapy but is reflected in other approaches, e.g., rational-emotive therapy and reality therapy.

Summary

Psychotherapy is viewed best as a specialized interpersonal relationship formed when a counselor-therapist, in possession of the personal characteristics and an armamentarium of therapeutic methods sufficient to effect positive behavior change, introgresses the life space of the client in order to assist the client with the resolution of some problem of living. A comprehensive and, we dare say, truly effective system of psychotherapy requires a) the blending of the scholarly, ethical, and curative motives and b) the synthesizing of insight and action psychotherapies. Integrative counseling and psychotherapy seeks such union, synthesis, and comprehensiveness.

Having provided an introductory perspective in Chapter 1 and a philosophic-theoretical base for an integrative psychotherapy in Chapter 2, let us now turn to the more practical aspects of counseling and psychotherapy. Chapters 3, 4, and 5 will be devoted to the counseling-therapy process, the application of multidimensional integrative therapy, and the implications for training and practice, respectively.

3

The Counseling-Therapy
Process

This chapter is concerned with counseling and psychotherapy as a *time-sequence process* which may involve a single therapeutic encounter or a lengthy series of counseling interviews. The counseling-therapy process begins at the moment the counselor-therapist introgresses into the life space of the client and continues until the therapist ceases to function as a significant force in the client's psychological environment. In his endeavors to effect the client-desired change in behavior and personality, the counselor necessarily focuses on the client's *past* learning and experiences, his *present* personal-social-psychological-phenomenal-existential situation, and his *future* goals, expectations, and possibilities.

A number of events or stages emerge sequentially as the therapeutic encounter develops. The serial events that are observed in the process of counseling and therapy can be delineated in terms of: relationship parameters, behavioral analysis, goal formulation, counseling strategies and therapeutic methods, and goal satisfaction and termination.

The Facilitative Relationship

It is highly probable that Carl Rogers' historic statement of 1957 has generated more responses and reactions, both positive and negative, among psychotherapists than any other assertion made during the last twenty years. In that statement Rogers posited the following conditions as necessary and sufficient for therapeutic change in behavior and personality: 1) two persons, an incongruent, vulnerable, or anxious client and a congruent or integrated counselor-therapist, must be in psychological contact in an interpersonal relationship; 2) the counselor-therapist experiences unconditional positive regard for and empathic understanding of the client and attempts to communicate these attitudes to the client; and 3) the client perceives, to a minimal degree, that the counselor-therapist does really respect and understand him. We seriously question that these conditions are sufficient for effective therapy with all types of clients and problems, but the results of empirical investigations indicate that a counselor-client relationship marked by these parameters is the *sine qua non* of counseling and psychotherapy (e.g., Rogers & Dymond, 1954; Truax & Carkhuff, 1967; Truax & Mitchell, 1971). Operating from the position that a facilitative interpersonal relationship is a necessary but insufficient condition for effecting the desired behavior change in all therapeutic encounters, the statements that follow represent my comprehension and appreciation of the relationship between counselor-therapist and client. Rather than being a mere stage in the therapy process, the relationship is *established early* in and *sustained throughout* the process.

The Initial Contact

The therapeutic encounter commences the moment the life spaces of the counselor-therapist and client intersect. The manner in which the counselor approaches the client in the early minutes of the counseling process can either "make" or "break" the relationship. The smile, the handshake, the sincere, warm, and friendly "hello," and the accepting, approving communication of the eyes — or the lack of these — have tremendous potential as reinforcers of interpersonal behaviors. Many clients come to counseling and psychotherapy "running scared" and very much need these therapeutic touches of social grace. The client needs to feel that the counselor is expressing verbally and nonverbally, "You're good and I like you." We speculate that a goodly number of clients terminate after the first interview due to the "cold shoulder" treatment they received in the opening minutes of the session.

The counselor should endeavor to make it easy for the client to get into the counseling-therapy room and become comfortable and relaxed. The walk from the lounge or waiting room to the counselor's office sometimes can be difficult and painful. Similarly, getting adjusted to and feeling safe in the counseling setting/situation is not without its moments of frustration.

It is important that the counselor-therapist demonstrate in a casual way a sense of poise, self-confidence, and professional competence to the client. But an air of artificial dignity, pompousness, and practiced professionalism has no place in the therapeutic encounter. Too, the client needs to feel early in the encounter that the therapist is profoundly interested in him as a person and sincerely desires to assist him with his concern in life. Any clues which suggest to the client that the counselor-therapist is experiencing irritation, boredom, disgust, or disinterest can do irreparable damage to the building of rapport.

Coping with Resistance

Typically, an individual enters counseling and psychotherapy with ambivalent feelings. On the one hand, the client sincerely wants to change some aspect of his personality and behavior and solicits the therapist's help with this task; but, on the other hand, the client is resistant to change and opposes the idea of therapy. To admit the need for counseling and therapy suggests weakness, dependency, inadequacy, and incompetence which are intolerable in a society based on the success-efficiency-independent self-sufficiency model. Another source of resistance arises from the tendency of the client to avoid the confronting of his feelings, especially intense negative feelings and those marked by strong attraction to that which is culturally taboo. Such resistance and split-motivation are true even in the self-referred client but are particularly evident in the client who enters therapy through the suggestion or action of an intermediary.

The counselor-client relationship will be enhanced if the counselor is able to exhibit patience, kindness, and tolerance as the client struggles with resistance. Furthermore, the counselor-therapist should manifest that he has an appreciation for the client's ambivalence, realizing that 1) it is not easy to receive help, 2) it is difficult to commit one's self to behavioral and personality change, 3) submitting to the influence of a professional helper poses as a threat to one's esteem, integrity, and independence, and 4) it is not easy to trust a stranger and to be open with him (Brammer, 1973). If the client can perceive the counselor as a compassionate human being, this will encourage him to move from resistance to trust and commitment.

Orienting the Client to Counseling and Therapy

Individuals who enter counseling and therapy for the first time, or those clients who seek the help of a therapist previously unknown to them, have little or no knowledge of what to expect. Thus, the uncertainty of the unknown and unexperienced produces anxiety or "stage fright" in the client. There are a number of things that the counselor can do to abet the creation of an effective relationship.

In the first place, the counselor can communicate to the client that he envisions their working together as equal human beings in an I - Thou dialogue. Although the therapist is in the position to be of help to the client, this does not imply that he is superior to the client in any form or fashion. Nor does the therapist have any power or authority over the client. Rather, the therapeutic encounter is premised on the right of the client to be in charge of his own life; therefore, the counselor-therapist assures the client that no efforts will be made to coerce, cajole, or control him. The counselor expresses that his chief concern is to be able to help the client achieve the status in life to which he aspires.

The counselor-therapist lets the client know that he is perceived and accepted as a "normal" human being who is struggling to adjust to life just as all other persons do. Yes, some problem in living has brought him to a counselor for help, but this does not mean that he is "sick," "abnormal," or "mentally ill." Instead, his situation is explicable in that it stems principally from unmet needs and inappropriate learning. Hopefully, as the therapeutic encounter progresses, the client will gain both an understanding of his situation and the strategies and skills necessary to alter it to his satisfaction.

The therapist shares with the client that there is nothing "magical" about psychotherapy. The therapist himself is simply a human being who has learned how to cope effectively with life and is in possession of the means to assist others with their concerns. Regarding the client's situation, his personality style and behavior patterns are learned phenomena, and psychotherapy will be essentially the provision of new and favorable conditions for therapeutic learning. Just as the client was actively involved in the learning of inappropriate and ineffective behaviors in the past, he will now become actively involved in the learning of new and more effective modes of behavior. The counselor assures the client that he will be beside him all the way in the process of therapy, but the client must assume a large part of the responsibility in achieving success in the therapeutic encounter. In other words, there is very little that the counselor can "do for or to" the client to make his life different and better — psychotherapy is a cooperative effort. In essence, the counselor is saying: "I believe in you, and I believe in myself, and *together* we can make your life to become what you want it to become." This kind of communication helps to foster self-confidence in the client as well as strengthen his confidence and trust in the therapist.

Providing Structure

A meaningful, workable, and productive interpersonal relationship depends, in part, on a mutual understanding of the roles, expectations, responsibilities, commitments, and limits of both client and counselor-therapist in the encounter. Thus, some form of *structuring* is a prerequisite for a truly effective counselor-client relationship. Among the specific elements to be considered in the structuring process, the following are illustrative ones: 1) the amount of time to be devoted to each interview and to the total counseling process; 2) the general procedures that will be followed in the process, with a special focus on the counselor-therapist's basic *modus operandi* and the client's feeling comfortable with this "plan of attack"; 3) the making and keeping of counseling appointments; and 4) if fees are involved, an early agreement should be reached regarding the amount per interview, and the manner and time of remittance. Such structure gives clarity and stability to the relationship, thus sparing the client unnecessary ambiguity, confusion, and anxiety.

Handling Transference

The instant in which the counselor-therapist enters the client's perceptual field, the client begins to experience specific feelings toward the therapist. These *transferred* feelings may be either positive or negative and are *real components* of the counselor-client relationship, not mere projections of historical imagos. The client's feelings toward the therapist may interfere with therapy, just as any other variable may do, but they need not, if they can be accepted in terms of what they really are. The answer to the question of transference is found, I believe, in the synthesis of learning theory and existential analysis.

This writer concurs with Dollard and Miller (1950) that transference in the therapeutic encounter is a special form of generalized learning. The therapist's presence as another human being creates a *social situation* much like those in which the client has previously been punished or rewarded by parents, teachers, and other significant persons. Thus, the *stimuli* of the counselor-therapist *provoke* the very same responses from the client which were learned in interaction with the significant figures of earlier life. If the counselor is perceived as a kind, compassionate, and supportive person, he will evoke the feelings of love and affection from the client. But if he appears to be forceful, manipulative, and punitive, the client will react with anger, hostility, and resistance.

Therefore, it behooves the counselor to be aware of the influence which his personality and behavior have on the relationship. The counselor should endeavor to provide a permissive atmosphere in which the client can express his true and real feelings without fear of being judged or punished. If the client's "transferred" feelings are mature and adaptive in nature, they can be experienced and enjoyed by both client and therapist. When the client's feelings toward the counselor appear to be unrealistic, inappropriate, or counter-productive, they should be explored in order a) to give the client a fuller understanding of himself and b) to make the relationship more mature and more workable.

The transference of positive feelings may be viewed as the expression of a genuine love relationship between the client and the counselor-therapist (Boss, 1963). The client begins to love the counselor-therapist as soon as he realizes that he has found someone — possibly for the first time in his life — who really understands and accepts him just as he is. The client loves the therapist all the more because he is permitted, within a safe interpersonal relationship, to unfold more fully his real and essential being. The client senses that the counselor-therapist is truly for him and has taken an authentic position of being-in-the-world with him.

Perhaps counselors and psychotherapists would be wise, as Boss has suggested, to do away altogether with the term "countertransference" and to replace it with the term "psychotherapeutic eros." Nothing could be more effective in building a relationship than the counselor's responding with genuine therapeutic love to the unique existence of the client. Thus, a reciprocal love relationship between client and counselor is posited as the viable replacement for the transference-countertransference model.

Demonstrating Love

We postulate that the entire process of counseling and psychotherapy, not just the "transference-countertransference" exchange of affect, is truly the practice of altruistic love. It appears, however, that psychotherapists who are devotees of rigorous empiricism have shunned serious study of love for two basic reasons: 1) many love phenomena are not easily observed and quantified in external reality so as to give them scientific respectability and clarity; and 2) the prevalent views of love in Western culture have been derived from the Hebraic-Christian tradition and this metaphysical influence prohibits love from achieving a reputable status in an empirical system. Be this as it may, it is obvious to the open-minded examiner that the counselor attitudes and behaviors which have been shown to be necessary for therapeutic gain clearly portray the phenomena of love.

The origin of the therapeutic conditions conducive to client gain can be traced to the unique contributions of four Greek terms for love which have molded psychotheological thought in the Western world: first, there is *agape* which refers to the unconditional and unselfish concern for and devotion to the welfare of another; second, *eros* reflects the individual's striving for union, being, meaning, and relationship; third, *philia* expresses one's feelings of friendship or brotherhood toward another human being; and fourth, *storge* represents the affection and good feelings one individual holds toward another person. Every aspect of the counseling process reflects in some measure one or more of these dimensions of love.

Incorporating the contributions of the preceding concepts and drawing from the ideas of a number of individuals (e.g., Prescott, 1952; Fromm, 1963; Sorokin, 1967; Truax & Carkhuff, 1967; May, 1969; Montagu, 1970a, 1970b; Shostrom, 1972), the following attempt is made toward defining the facilitative relationship as the practice and demonstration of genuine love. Instead of a passive emotionalism, love is conceived as a composite of internal states (attitudes, feelings, valuings, reactions, and responses) and overt behaviors which the counselor-therapist manifests through purposeful action in relating to the client. Specifically, the counselor-therapist demonstrates therapeutic love by:

Understanding, accepting, liking, enjoying, disclosing, and authentically being himself — being integrated, congruent, and genuine.

Possessing unconditional positive regard, respect, or nonpossessive warmth for the client *and* effectively communicating these attitudes to the client.

Causing the client-person to feel or sense that he has intrinsic worth, dignity, and ability through the unconditional caring for him.

Understanding and experiencing deeply and accurately the feelings, concerns, and experiences of the client — communicating concretely that you comprehend the client's existential situation and are standing in his world with him.

Providing a non-threatening, trusting, and safe atmosphere for the client to engage in self-disclosure, self-exploration, and self-determination.

Encouraging, allowing, and assisting the client to choose his own goals to work toward in the counseling process (to be discussed more fully in a later section).

Affirming a professional preparedness and personal willingness to use any ethical method, procedure, or technique to help, support, and fulfill the needs, interests, and goals of the client.

Convincing the client of a profound interest in his welfare and a sincere desire to become personally involved in his life and to remain so involved for as long an amount of time as is necessary to resolve his conflict, problem, or concern.

Seeking whatever is best for the client with no desire or intention to give the consistency of a theoretical system a higher priority than his concerns.

Continually examining the effectiveness of the counseling strategy and having concern enough to make any necessary adjustments or adaptations throughout the therapy process.

Summary

An egalitarian relationship between the counselor-therapist and client is posited as the desired social matrix for the counseling process. The relationship is marked by a warm, permissive atmosphere with the nonjudgmental therapist accepting the client as he is and reflects the Hebraic-Christian virtues of faith, hope, and love. Specifically, the therapeutic encounter can be perceived best as the practice of genuine love which is demonstrated through the counselor-therapist's attitudes and actions regarding the person and situation of the client. These factors are accepted as the necessary, but not sufficient, conditions for effective counseling and psychotherapy.

Behavioral Analysis

When counseling and psychotherapy first became a formalized practice, diagnosis occupied a central position. But interest in the diagnostic function has declined during the last quarter century due primarily to the widespread influence of humanistic psychology, especially the client-centered view. Exponents of the client-centered approach have argued vigorously and consistently that the judgmental nature of medical model-oriented diagnosis, with its emphasis on symptoms and etiology, is detrimental to the client-counselor relationship and, therefore, is inimical to constructive change in the personality of the client. But diagnosis need not be construed so negatively nor be held in such a limited perspective.

In the integrative approach to counseling and psychotherapy, room is made for the diagnostic function without the disease connotation and nosological labels. Diagnosis or behavioral analysis is understood to be essentially the thorough understanding, knowledge, or discernment which the counselor-therapist has regarding the client's personal-social-psychological-phenomenal-existential situation. The position advocated here postulates a valid diagnosis or behavioral analysis as the prerequisite to intelligent, indeed, effective counseling and psychotherapy. If clients are different and if the problems and concerns they bring to the counselor-therapist are different, then "differential" diagnoses or analyses and differential modes of therapy are demanded. Therapy must be adapted to the uniqueness of each counseling situation.

A guide to behavioral analysis, the components of which reflect the pattern followed by action-oriented therapists (e.g., Wolpe & Lazarus, 1966; Kanfer & Saslow, 1969; Kanfer & Phillips, 1970; Osipow & Walsh, 1970), is offered here as a workable model to be followed in diagnosing presenting problems. The analytic model presented here does not intend to assign the client to diagnostic categories. Instead, it is designed to serve as a basis for making decisions about specific therapeutic interventions, regardless of the nature of the presenting problem. The compilation of data under the suggested headings should provide a good basis for decisions about the areas in which intervention is needed, the specific targets of the intervention, the therapeutic methods to be used, and the goal or series of goals at which the counseling-therapy process should aim. (This analytic or diagnostic model is complementary to our concept of problematic behavior which was developed in Chapter 2.)

Preliminary Analysis of the Problem Situation

The initial task is to discover what the presenting problem really is. Except in existential crises, problems in living arise from either the individual's performing inappropriately or his inability to perform the desired behaviors. Thus, a preliminary formulation attempts to sort or categorize the client's major complaints into classes of *behavioral excesses* and *deficits.* Some client behaviors are described as problematic because of excess in their frequency, intensity, duration, or occurrence under conditions which are not socially acceptable. Other behaviors are considered by the client to be problematic because they fail to occur with sufficient frequency, with adequate intensity, in appropriate form, or under socially approved conditions. In terms of content, the response or behavior categories represent the primary targets of the therapeutic intervention. That is, these classes of complaints suggest the particular problems to be focused on in the counseling-therapy process.

Clarification of the Problem Situation

The preliminary analysis of the problem behavior usually leaves many loose ends to be pulled together and clarified. In the second phase of behavioral analysis an effort is made to ascertain the specific variables that maintain the client's current problematic behaviors. The focus is on the people and circumstances which seem to affect the disturbing behaviors, and the consequences which these behaviors have for the client and for significant others in his life. Also, a clearer understanding is sought of the specific conditions under which the problematic behavior occurs. Thus, the analysis zeroes in on stimulus conditions, significant others, and the environmental events (psychological, social, biological, economic, vocational, etc.) associated with the occurrence of specific coping behavior excesses and deficiencies. Knowledge of the presenting problem(s) is moved out of the realm of general vagueness to where the situation is comprehended in a much clearer perspective. The result is a firmer grasp of the exact nature of the problem and what might be done to modify the situation.

Developmental Analysis

Since the client's present situation is influenced by his past learnings and experiences, it is important that attention be given to the client's developmental history. Analysis of the developmental history provides a means for discovering inappropriate learning and unmet basic human needs. A profile of the client's characteristic personal-behavioral development can be acquired by exploring his family environment, his sociocultural matrix, his medical history, his educational history, his occupational history, and his psychosexual history. A developmental analysis provides a fuller comprehension of both the client's assets and his deficiencies and suggests how his potential range of coping behaviors has been limited, as well as how it might be increased in the counseling-therapy process. With a given client, special attention should be directed to particular aspects of the developmental history and others possibly omitted.

Analysis of the Existential Status and Self-Control

Here the focus is on the self-concept of the client, his ego strength, and his ability to manage the affairs of his life. Does he have realistic perceptions of himself and his world or are they too idealistic or self-defeating? What is the morale and motivational status of the client — does life have meaning and value for him? In what situations can the client control his problematic behavior and how does he achieve control? Are there any conditioned approach and avoidance reactions evidenced in the client's present behaviors? What is the nature of his ideological-attitudinal reactions, social roles, and life style patterns? This section of the analysis further defines the client and his problem situation, indicates the client's capacity to participate in a therapeutic encounter, and suggests the strategy to be followed.

Analysis of the Environmental Press

Focal here are the client's social relationships with significant people in his current environment and the expectations and limitations with which he must contend. The client's social network (home, church, school, work, clubs, social groups, etc.) is investigated in order a) to assess the significance of individuals in the client's present environment who have some influence — positive and negative — over his problem behavior and b) to plan the potential participation of these significant others in the counseling-therapy process, if it appears that their involvement would be facilitative in effecting the desired client change. Too, the client's behavior is assessed against the background of the norms prevalent in his natural environment, and the agreements and discrepancies between the client's life patterns and the norms in the environment are reviewed. This analysis is very important since the goals for the counseling-therapy process must allow explicitly both for the client's needs and for the pressures of his social environment.

Some Concluding Remarks

First, the more intense or serious in nature a presenting problem appears to be, the greater is the amount of attention that is given to etiology and the analysis of behavior. Second, behavioral analysis is in no way a violation of the client-counselor relationship; rather, it is an extension of the relationship. Third, although the problem and its causes may be identified early in the counseling-therapy process, new dimensions of the problem will unfold as the therapeutic encounter progresses, leading to re-analysis of the problematic behavior. Fourth, may it suffice to say that the client, not the problem *per se,* remains the center of attention in behavioral analysis — the efforts made to comprehend thoroughly the client's situation reflects the counselor-therapist's deep interest in the client as a person. Finally, behavioral analysis prepares the way for the formulation of concrete counseling goals and for the intelligent selection of the appropriate therapeutic methods and strategies.

Goal Formulation

Behavioral analysis shows what is wrong with the client's personal world but is insufficient in itself to provide the direction of and the objective for therapeutic movement. The establishment of specific counseling goals or objectives necessarily follow the identification of the problem and the assessment of its etiology.

Mahrer (1967) speculates that the goals of counseling and psychotherapy in general can be placed in six major categories. In some therapeutic encounters the goal is to reduce psychopathology by removing symptomatic and/or defensive behaviors. A second widely observed counseling objective is the reduction of psychological pain and suffering such as anxiety, hostility, meaninglessness, and loneliness. Many counseling relationships seek to increase pleasure in the client through fostering self-fulfillment, a sense of organismic well-being, and positive feelings about life. A fourth type of counseling-therapy goal is concerned with increased client experiencing—assisting the client to feel alive, to have a vital sense of being, to possess openness and commitment, to experience concretely the process of living and feeling. Other therapeutic encounters work toward an enhanced self-relationship — that is, the client achieves an increased self-acceptance, self-appreciation, and internal directedness. Finally, the objective of many counselor-client involvements is to enhance the client's external relationships such as building better or closer interpersonal relationships, increasing one's competence to function effectively, acquiring greater ability to adjust to the environment, and establishing more effective social skills. A comprehensive psychotherapy allows for all these counseling objectives instead of following a certain one prescriptively.

It is easy, however, for the counselor-therapist to assume one of the preceding goal-types as *the* objective for the counseling-therapy process. For example, orthodox psychoanalysis and client-centered psychotherapy invariably perceive the goal of therapy to be the lifting or removal of repressed unconscious material and becoming a congruent, fully-functioning person, respectively. Although these are worthy goals, it is inappropriate for the counselor to assume them on an a priori basis.

Integrative counseling and psychotherapy approaches the formulation of counseling goals in similar fashion as do behavioral counselor-therapists (e.g., Krumboltz, 1966; Krumboltz & Thoresen, 1969). Five principal criteria govern the establishment of goals for the counseling-therapy process: 1) the goal must be desired by the client, rather than originating from the counselor; 2) the goal must be stated differently and uniquely for each individual client and in concrete terms understood by the client; 3) the counseling goal should be compatible with, though not necessarily identical to, the values of the counselor-therapist; 4) the counselor-therapist must both sense that he is professionally competent and be genuinely willing to assist the client to achieve his goal; and 5) it must be possible to observe to what extent the client achieves his goal. A goal or set of goals for the counseling process which meets these criteria is both scientific and humanistic.

Thus, the establishment of a goal for the counseling process is client-centered rather than stemming from the theoretical predisposition of the counselor-therapist. We might add that often it is necessary for the therapist to help the client state the counseling goal, but the goal is never imposed nor assumed by the therapist. This gives further indication that the counselor-therapist possesses genuine respect for the integrity and capability of the client.

Therapeutic Methods and Strategies

It was asserted above that the facilitative relationship is necessary but insufficient for truly effective counseling and psychotherapy with all clients and all types of problems. The therapist must be in possession of an armamentarium of therapeutic methods with which to supplement the counselor-client interpersonal encounter. Neither the relationship nor the application of therapeutic methods alone accounts for success in the counseling process. Rather, the client gains results from the combination of relationship parameters and the well-timed, skillful use of appropriate counseling techniques and strategies. While the components of an effective relationship have a basic sameness for all counselor-client encounters, the selection of therapeutic methods varies with the uniqueness of each client-problem situation. Among other variables, the nature of the presenting problem, the nature of the counseling goal, and the personal-psychological-existential status of the client determine the appropriateness of a particular mode of therapy in a given case or at a given time in the counseling process. No single therapeutic method exists which can be employed as the exclusive and sufficient strategy either with all clients or with the same client all the time. Differential modes of therapy are just as essential to a comprehensive system of counseling and psychotherapy as are differential behavioral analyses and individualized counseling objectives.

Identified below are a number of therapeutic methods, techniques, and procedures deemed by the writer to be a) complementary to the philosophic-theoretical conceptualizations developed in Chapter 2, b) supplementary to the other elements of the counseling-therapy process which are presented in this chapter, and c) compatible with the life style of the writer-therapist. For pragmatic purposes, the techniques and procedures are discussed under the "schools" (arranged alphabetically) with which they are *most closely* associated, and only the "unique" contributions of each school are included. Variations of certain techniques, e.g., the handling of dreams, are utilized by different schools of counseling and psychotherapy. In such instances, the variant that best fits the philosophic-theoretical world view of the writer will be incorporated.

Adlerian Contributions

Encouragement

In many instances clients suffer from discouragement, a sense of failure, and the loss of hope both in themselves and in life. The counselor-therapist can employ encouragement as a primary technique with these individuals. The therapist's expression of belief/faith/confidence in the client, his noncondemnation of him, his avoidance of being overly demanding of him, his standing as an equal and understanding friend with the client, and his helping the client to attempt some course of action he has feared or did not know was available to him, all combine to restore a sense of self-confidence and a feeling of hope in the client (Mosak & Dreikurs, 1973). The client needs to believe in himself, and to do so, he must first have someone else who believes in him.

Gamesmanship Tactics

Clients often engage in neurotic, manipulative moves in the therapy encounter. The alert and circumspective counselor-therapist can counter these moves therapeutically with gamesmanship tactics. For example, in order to claim uniqueness and to challenge the counselor's ability to help him, the client might say, "I bet you have never seen a client like me." An effective response by the therapist could be, "No, not since the interview which I completed in the last hour." Or the client might declare, "I have seen so many therapists that you are my last hope in life." The counselor could counter the neurotic claim to superiority with, "No, I'm not the last hope. Perhaps there may be others who can help you too" (Adler, 1964). In his efforts to help melancholics cultivate social interest, Adler (1964) would use statements such as "Don't tax yourself, do only what you find interesting and agreeable." Should the client's response be something like, "But, nothing is interesting and agreeable to me," Adler would counter with: "Then at least do not exert yourself to do what is disagreeable." Such gamesmanship tactics not only defuse the client's intentions but also prepare the way for a more productive therapeutic dialogue.

Life-Style Analysis

The individual brings to the counseling-therapy setting a dissatisfying life-style which is founded on fictitious goals, mistaken apperceptions, and unrealistic coping strategies. The counselor-therapist begins to try to understand the client's style of life from the first moment of the therapeutic encounter. The client's manner of walking, his posture, how and where he sits, and his communication patterns, all provide indices to an understanding of the client's law of movement. But of chief importance to life-style analysis are the investigations of the family constellation and early recollections of the client. These investigations ascertain the conditions prevailing when the individual was forming his life-style convictions or laying down a prototypical life plan of action. Data may be gathered by methods ranging from a formal inventory (e.g., Mosak & Shulman, 1971) to the therapist's inviting the client to narrate his "Story of My Life." An examination of the client's psychological position within his family and of his earliest memories in life reveals a) his perceptions of himself and others, b) his mistaken conceptions and assumptions (basic mistakes) about life, c) the determinants or dynamics of his movement in life, and d) how the life-style affects his current striving to fulfill the tasks of life — social, work, love (sex), spiritual (cosmological or ontological), and self (subjective and objective).

Interpretation

Insight into the client's self-deceptive and dissatisfying style of life is facilitated chiefly by interpretation. The emphasis is on the client's present goals, intentions, purposes, and movement rather than on causative dynamics, descriptive analyses, and the past. The client is perceived as strong rather than fragile and is confronted with his goals, intentions, neurotic symptoms, fantasies, dreams, behaviors, and modes of relating and communicating interpersonally. Interpretation then is essentially a mirror which the counselor-therapist holds up so the client can explore his values, perceive the purpose of his behavior, see how he copes with life's tasks, comprehend the basic premise of his life-style, interpret his own situation, draw his own conclusions, and become aware of his responsibility in the decisions he makes and must make regarding the direction of his life.

A thorough life-style investigation that is interpreted accurately and effectively to the client results in insight which leads to a reorientation to life. A new style of living characterized by social interest, realistic goals, and responsible living emerges to replace a self-defeating one marked by feelings of inferiority, neurotic self-absorption, and fictional finalism.

Behavioral Contributions

Positive Reinforcement

Rather than being a single technique, positive reinforcement connotes a class of behavior strategies which belong to the operant conditioning model. When the counselor-therapist employs the operant conditioning paradigm in the counseling process, he presumes that if the client's behavior is followed by immediate positive reinforcement or reward, the probability of the behavior occurring again is increased (Skinner, 1953). Specifically, the counselor-therapist uses verbal responses, valued objects, social recognition, and client-preferred activities to reinforce and modify systematically desired client behaviors. Among the many potential reinforcers, verbal reinforcement or conditioning appears to be indispensable to the therapeutic encounter and is present, whether intentional or otherwise, in some form in virtually all approaches to counseling and psychotherapy.

The counselor-therapist who is well acquainted with these positive reinforcement techniques operates from an advantaged position. He can either use them within the counseling sessions to reinforce in-session behaviors, or serve as a consultant/collaborator to/with other persons in the client's life, such as a teacher or parent, who can complement the counseling-therapy goals with a program of reinforcement of behaviors outside the therapy setting.

Role-Playing or Behavioral Rehearsal

Role-playing or behavior rehearsal has many variations but consists essentially of the acting out of exchanges between the counselor-therapist and the client concerning anxiety provoking situations in the client's world or life (Krumboltz & Thoresen, 1969; Wolpe, 1973). The immediate objective of role-playing is to enable a client to rehearse a new or more effective mode of behavior as often as necessary without anxiety about its consequences. The client is reinforced in a two-fold manner: in the first place, he is encouraged by the positive feedback he receives from the counselor-therapist for the improvement he makes toward his goal; secondly, the client is reinforced as he gains confidence in his own ability to change or improve. The ultimate aim of role-playing is, of course, to prepare the client to live or function without self-defeating fears and anxieties in his real world. Thus, for role-playing to be of maximal effectiveness, it should be conducted under conditions which approximate those found in the client's *in vivo* situations.

Assertive Training

This counter conditioning technique rests on behavior rehearsal and the principle of reciprocal inhibition and is particularly useful with clients who are submissive, deferent, and can't stand up for themselves. Wolpe (1973) defines reciprocal inhibition thus: "If a response inhibiting anxiety can be made to occur in the presence of anxiety-evoking stimuli, it will weaken the bond between these stimuli and the anxiety" (p. 17). Assertive training begins with the client identifying a situation in which he wishes to be assertively expressive either in his feelings or his ideas. The situation is then rehearsed with the counselor-therapist consistently in the interview setting until the client can be assertive without experiencing any anxiety. Each act of assertion reciprocally inhibits, to some extent, the client's experiencing of anxiety and slightly weakens the anxiety-response habit — the client cannot be assertive and anxiously avoiding simultaneously. The positive feelings which the client experiences toward himself as he behaves assertively also reciprocally inhibit anxiety. *In vivo* practice of the rehearsed assertive behaviors supplements and speeds up the in-session therapy. Eventually, the individual will be able to actualize fully his assertive self in his total world.

Systematic Desensitization

This technique, too, is based on the principle of reciprocal inhibition and employs relaxation as the counter conditioning agent with clients suffering from noninterpersonal anxiety neuroses. More specifically, systematic desensitization is the breaking down, step by step, of neurotic anxiety-response habits by first inducing a state of relaxation in the client and then exposing him to a weak anxiety-arousing stimulus. Relaxation is reciprocally inhibitory of anxiety and, if the exposure to the anxiety-evoking stimulus is repeated several times while the client is in a relaxed state, the stimulus loses its ability to arouse anxiety. In the process of desensitization, progressively stronger stimuli are introduced and treated similarly until the strongest anxiety-provoking stimulus is experienced without any anxiety. Thus, for desensitization to be effective, three things are essential: the client must be capable of 1) relaxing totally and deeply and 2) experiencing vicariously and realistically noxious stimuli by imagining scenes or by viewing simulated anxiety-evoking situations and 3) the counselor-therapist, in collaboration with the client, must be able to construct relevant hierarchies of anxiety-arousing stimuli.

The techniques for inducing relaxation consist of learning to tense sequentially and then relax various groups of muscles all through the body, while at the same time paying attention to the feelings associated with both tension and relaxation (Bernstein & Borkovec, 1973). It is necessary for the client to concentrate on feeling relaxed and to focus his attention on various parts of his body until he feels totally and deeply relaxed. The desired physical setting includes a) a quiet, attractive, carpeted, dimly lighted room, b) a well-padded recliner or over-stuffed chair, and c) comfortable, loose-fitting clothing, preferably slacks and shirt/blouse. In-session training in progressive relaxation should be supplemented with practice of the skills outside the therapy encounter. (The reader is referred to Jacobson, 1938, and Bernstein & Borkovec, 1973, for detailed information regarding training in relaxation.)

Anxiety hierarchies are drawn up while the training in progressive relaxation is in progress, but not while the client is under relaxation. The data from which the hierarchies are constructed come from a) the client's social-psychological case history, b) his responses to psychological inventories and questionnaires such as the Willoughby Questionnaire and Fear Survey Schedule, and c) inquiries into situations in which the client feels excessive anxiety. The anxiety-arousing stimuli are categorized according to themes, and the stimuli of a common theme are then ranked in descending order in terms of the amount of anxiety they evoke. Woody (1971) has constructed an excellent example of a hierarchy of noxious stimuli for a college freshman who experiences test-taking anxiety:

1. Sitting in the front of the classroom, taking the examination with a professor watching him.
2. Sitting in the front of the classroom, taking the examination with a student-proctor observing.
3. Sitting in the back of the classroom, taking the examination with a professor at the front of the room.
4. Sitting in the back of the classroom, taking the examination with a student-proctor at the front of the room.
5. Approaching the classroom on the day an examination is to occur.
6. Studying in his dormitory room the night before an examination.
7. Studying in his dormitory room any time.
8. Studying in the library.
9. Seeing one of his professors on campus.
10. Thinking of the possibility of being tested. (p. 72)

When the anxiety hierarchy has been drawn up and the client is able to relax deeply, the desensitization procedure proper is begun. The therapist initiates the process by having the client relax and then imagine, with eyes closed, a neutral, pleasant situation or scene, such as reclining on a sofa before a glowing fireplace or lying on his back in a meadow watching the clouds move nonchalantly overhead. If the client is able to form and sustain a clear image, he indicates this with a raised finger. The client's ability to visualize anxiety-free situations assures the counselor-therapist that the client is capable of imagining scenes from the anxiety hierarchy. The client is now asked to imagine the least anxiety-evoking scene on the hierarchy and to raise his finger when he sees a clear image. The counselor-therapist allows the scene to remain for approximately 5–7 seconds and terminates it with, "Stop the scene." The client is asked to rate, using a scale of 0 to 100, how much anxiety he experienced. If the client states that no anxiety was experienced, relaxation is then induced again for 10–20 seconds, and the second scene is presented. (If necessary, the same scene will be repeated until the anxiety level has been reduced to zero.) The process continues for as many sessions required for the client to progress up the hierarchy of situations and to imagine the most anxiety-provoking scene without any anxiety. It is recommended that the client try exposing himself at various stages of the counseling-therapy process to *in vivo* situations up to which he has been desensitized. For example, an individual fearful of elevators could be asked to go out in real life and perform up to the last desensitized point. This serves at least three purposes: consolidates progress, provides feedback, and accelerates desensitization.

Modeling

Social modeling, sometimes called imitative, vicarious, or observational learning, is a versatile, yet fundamental, means of assisting clients with the acquisition of new modes of behavior and with the modification of existing behavioral patterns (Bandura, 1969). Modeling is essentially the counselor-therapist's providing an opportunity for the client to change his behavior by observing and imitating the behavior exhibited by another person. Modeling lends itself to a variety of formats. Live models may include the counselor himself, compeers of the client, or other socially desirable persons who demonstrate desired behaviors to the client. Or the behavior to be acquired or changed can be presented by symbolic models through video-tapes or films. Too, bibliotherapy materials and audio-tapes can be used to model specifically desired behaviors. These approaches may be used separately or in combinations to assist either an individual client or a group of clients. In some situations the therapist might deem it wise to use operant conditioning and positively reinforce the client for imitating the model's behavior. But in other cases, perhaps all that is required is the opportunity for the client to observe the model.

Contact Desensitization

This technique is suitable for use with a wide age range and is especially effective with individuals who suffer from avoidance behaviors and objective fears. Contact desensitization encompasses, among other operations, social modeling and operant conditioning and may be used either *in vivo* or vicariously. *In vivo* contact desensitization consists of the counselor-therapist a) serving as a live social model to demonstrate appropriate behaviors to the client, b) using physical contact with the client to aid in the modifying or shaping of his behavior, and c) employing positive reinforcers, verbal and nonverbal, to reward the client for making progress toward the counseling goal. The therapist presents the least difficult or threatening behaviors to the client in the early stages of the counseling-therapy process and gradually introduces the more difficult responses as the client gains proficiency in the lower order ones.

Ritter (1969) identifies the main components of contact desensitization as demonstration, counselor-contact, and client participation. The basic steps in the process may be defined as follows:

1. The counselor-therapist models or demonstrates the modes of behavior which he and the client have decided mutually as being relevant to the counseling objectives.

2. The counselor-therapist assists the client in imitating the modeled behavior by using physical contact such as holding the client's hand or arm while the client performs the feared behavior.

3. The counselor-therapist gradually withdraws the physical contact or support as the client progressively increases his independent practice of the desired behavior.

Aversion Therapy

Aversion therapy is a special application of the reciprocal inhibition principle in which an aversive stimulus is administered in temporal contiguity with a pleasant stimulus to inhibit an unwanted or undesirable emotional response or behavior. This method is particularly applicable to compulsive behavioral habits such as excessive drinking, overeating, smoking, homosexuality, fetishism, and transvestism (Lazarus, 1971; Wolpe, 1973). While a variety of techniques may be employed to implement this mode of therapy — electrical stimulation or shock, administering of nausea-producing drugs, etc. — this counselor-therapist accepts *aversive imagery* and/or *covert sensitization* as being more compatible with the approach to psychotherapy presented in this volume. Aversion therapy via aversive imagery consists of having the client to imagine a verbally suggested aversive response (e.g., nausea and painful, embarrassing vomiting) while being turned-on to a pleasant stimulus (e. g., food, cigarettes, homosexual companion) which is either real, pictorial, or imaginary. Covert sensitization is but an extended use of aversive imagery where the client is first relaxed and then asked to visualize the pleasurable object and when picturing himself ready to indulge, he is instructed to imagine an aversive response.

Client-Centered Contributions

Reflection

The counseling relationship alone serves adequately as the therapeutic method with certain clients — e.g., individuals with unwholesome self-concepts, intrapersonal conflict or incongruence, and/or poor interpersonal relationships. If the counselor-therapist is able to enter the client's internal frame of reference and be perceived by the client as being genuine, as having empathic understanding of him and an unconditional positive regard for him, then constructive change in the client's personality and behavior can be expected. The reflection of feelings and experiences constitutes the principal vehicle used by the client-centered therapist to facilitate client gain. More specifically, the counselor-therapist's technique of reflecting the client's feelings provides a technical channel for fulfilling the conditions of effective counseling and therapy. That is, the counselor-therapist promotes the desired client growth and change by communicating accurate empathy and genuine respect via reflective statements, clarifications, summarizations, and reformulations of the client's expressions. Through an over-time process of thinking, feeling, being, experiencing, and exploring with the client, the counselor-therapist works toward the client's moving *from* the status of a rigid, incongruent, and noncommunicative person who lives in the past, denying and distorting his feelings and experiences, *to* becoming an open, congruent, and fully functioning person who is able to live freely in the here and now as an integrated, feeling, experiencing organism (Rogers, 1961).

Existential-Logotherapeutic Contributions

Logotherapeutic Encounter

A common complaint of many people today is that their lives have no meaning at all. These individuals lack a philosophy of life and values adequate to motivate and give meaning to their personal existence. Consequently, they subsist in an existential vacuum and experience only emptiness, boredom, apathy, and frustration. Thus, many clients seek help with existential, philosophical, and spiritual problems. Rather than psychotherapy *per se,* it is logotherapy (Frankl 1962, 1965, 1969) that such clients need. The counselor-therapist enters an I – Thou relationship with the client and employs a maieutic, Socratic dialogue to assist the client in his search for the hidden *logos* (meaning) of his existence. Logotherapy as a specific therapy is neither preaching nor teaching; rather, it is an encounter between human beings in which one, the counselor-therapist, confronts the other, the client, with the meaning of being. Grist for the logotherapeutic encounter are: 1) the resolution of value conflicts; 2) explorations of the meaning of life, love, work, suffering, and death; 3) formulating a mature philosophy of life, including a personally satisfying set of values; 4) achieving a sense of individual uniqueness, freedom, and responsibleness, and 5) becoming committed to a meaningful mission in life. Although the logotherapeutic encounter seeks healing through meaning and value clarification, the counselor-therapist is careful not to impose or give meaning and values to the client; instead, he helps the client find his own meaning and values.

Paradoxical Intention

This technique is particularly useful in cases involving anticipatory anxiety. When a client reacts to an event with a fearful expectation of its recurrence, his anticipatory anxiety makes to happen that which he fears. Thus, the client finds himself in a vicious circle where a neurotic response or symptom produces a phobia and the phobia in turn provokes the symptom, and the recurrence of the symptom serves to reinforce the phobia (Frankl, 1969). The client then turns to his most effective mode of coping behavior, avoidance of the situations in which he expects his fears to recur.

The counselor-therapist intervenes with paradoxical intention and encourages the client to modify his behavior by intending, doing, or wishing for that which he anticipates with fear. This method closely resembles the behavioral principle of reciprocal inhibition. In essence, paradoxical intention is the inhibiting of an anxious response by intending it. The fearful expectation or anticipatory anxiety is defused/inhibited by a paradoxical wish. Furthermore, the client cannot take flight from his fear while intending it. As Frankl has postulated, this technique rests on man's existential capacities of self-transcendence and self-detachment — man is able to stand outside of his neurosis and then conquer his situation by arising humorously and defiantly above it.

De-reflection

De-reflection also rests on the existential-logotherapeutic principle of self-transcendence and is designed to neutralize compulsive self-observation or hyper-reflection, and hyper-intention. It is possible for an individual, in his struggle to find pleasure in life and/or to overcome obsessive-compulsive behaviors, to be progressively more overwhelmed by his symptoms. In other words, the client tries so hard to be successful that he ends up a greater "failure." The counselor-therapist seeks to de-reflect the client from his anticipatory anxiety to something more positive. Through de-reflection, the client is enabled to ignore his problem by turning his attention away from himself. He learns to replace "wrong activity" with "right activity" as he is directed toward altruistic living in which he finds personal meaning and satisfaction.

Gestalt Contributions

Rules

Rules are *not* a list of dogmatic *do's* and *don'ts* to regulate behavior; rather they are experimental devices that can be employed in the therapeutic encounter to assist the client to make better contact with himself and his environment. They are designed to a) help deal with resistances, b) promote increased awareness and fuller experiencing, c) facilitate growth and motivation, and d) unify thought and feeling (Levitsky & Perls, 1970). Following is an identification of the Gestalt rules.

HERE AND NOW: Communications in the present tense are encouraged in order to promote *now* awareness. The client's past is important, but the most effective means of integrating past material into the personality is to bring it, as fully as possible, into the present. Indeed, the relevant past *is* present in the here and now of the client's existence. For example, the memories an individual has of an unresolved emotional event are very much alive in his *now*, and the Gestalt can be completed only through reliving and experiencing the historical situation in the existential now.

I AND THOU: True communication and interpersonal experiencing involves the *I* of the sender making direct, personal contact with the *Thou* of the receiver. When a client "talks at" rather than "talking to" the intended receiver of his message, he is challenged to face his avoidance of relating directly to/making genuine contact with others. This enables the client to become aware of the basic nature of his interpersonal relations — he begins to perceive whether he is truly with people or feels alienated and alone, whether other people are important to him or do not really exist in his world.

I LANGUAGE: The client who refers to his body and to his behaviors in objective, second and third person, *you*-and-*it* language is asked to substitute "I" for "you" and "it." This facilitates the individual's perceiving himself as an active, dynamic agent rather than a passive, acted-upon creature. "I" expressions help the client to get in touch with himself and enhance his sense of personal responsibility, involvement, and control regarding his total behavior.

WHAT AND HOW OF BEHAVIOR: The client can best gain a knowledge of himself through an awareness of his feelings, sensations, perceptions rather than by intellectualizations, explanations, and interpretations. Therefore, the counselor-therapist focuses on the *what* and *how* of behavior — the so-called "awareness continuum" — in order to guide the client to a real awareness and experiencing of his sensorimotor self and away from the interpretive *why* of behavior. For example, should the client say, "I feel frustrated," an appropriate counselor response would be, "How do you experience the frustration?" — rather than, "Why are you frustrated?"

GOSSIPING, VERBOTEN: Often in group counseling a client will "gossip" or "talk about" a member of the group rather than addressing the member directly. Generally, the client gossips about an individual because he is unable to cope effectively with the feelings that person provokes in him. The therapist uses the "no-gossiping" rule to facilitate direct confrontation of the client's feelings. To illustrate, Jim and Sherri are members of a group; Sherri looks in the direction of the counselor-therapist and says, "I get angry with Jim because he is so domineering." The therapist asks Sherri, "Can you tell Jim how you feel?" Sherri then turns to face Jim and expresses, "Jim, the way you try to dominate the group angers me."

STATEMENTS VERSUS QUESTIONS: Many of the questions asked in the counseling-therapy encounter are unnecessary and undesirable. Rather than serving as genuinely helpful and supportive measures, questions frequently represent passivity, laziness, lack of involvement, manipulation, cajoling, and/or indirect advice-giving on the part of the client. The counselor-therapist asks the client to change an inappropriate question into a statement in order to optimize communication, awareness, and experience in the therapeutic encounter.

Games

Closely related to the Gestalt rules are scores of games or exercises which the counselor-therapist may propose as therapeutic devices at appropriate times in the therapy process. Following are a few representative examples of the many games that may be used to facilitate self-awareness and personality growth.

DIALOGUE: In virtually every counseling situation the individual experiences some type of discordant polarization in his personality functioning. Typical splits or dualisms are masculine versus feminine, agressive versus passive, strong versus weak, commanding versus resisting, and desirable versus undesirable. When the counselor-therapist picks up the discordant poles in the personality of the client, one strategy he uses to effect integrated functioning of the fragmented parts is having the client engage the two disagreeing components of himself in actual dialogue. The discordant parts confront each other, vis-a-vis, until the two elements merge into a new, balanced realization (Kempler, 1973). The dialogue may be between a) two differing psychological attitudes or feelings, b) two parts or sections of the body, or c) between the personality of the client and some significant other person whose personality clashes with that of the client. In group settings, members of the group may identify with either of the two poles and enter the dialogue.

MAKING THE ROUNDS: In some instances the counselor-therapist may sense that the client's awareness and discovery of self would be enhanced should he express a particular thought or feeling to each person in the group, individually, making pertinent amplifications with each repetition. Should a client remark, "I feel uncomfortable in this group," he could be asked to verbalize this statement vis-a-vis every other person in the group, adding other words to communicate his particular feelings about each individual. Making the rounds may involve, in addition to verbal interaction, touching, caressing, observing, and various forms of dramatization.

COMPLETING UNFINISHED BUSINESS: Clients bring unfinished business or unresolved feelings — hurt, anger, guilt, resentment — to the therapy setting. When unfinished business surfaces in the counseling-therapy process, the client is asked to complete the task by acting- or living-it-out in the here and now. Role-playing, psychodrama, and "pillow therapy" are some special methods for helping with the resolution of unresolved feelings.

PLAYING THE PROJECTION: Quite often what is understood by the client to be a perception is really a projection. That is, a trait, attitude, feeling, or mode of behavior which actually belongs to the client's personality but is not experienced as such, is attributed to another person and then experienced as directed *toward* him by the other person rather than vice versa (Perls, Hefferline & Goodman, 1951). Whenever a client expresses a projection disguised as a perception, he is encouraged to play the role of the person involved in the projection to discover his own conflict in this area. For example, a client who says to the counselor-therapist, "You don't really care about me," may be asked to play the role of a non-caring person. After the role-playing, the client could be asked to examine himself to see whether this is a "disowned" trait he himself possesses.

REVERSALS: The reversal technique is used to help the client realize that overt or manifest behavior often represents the reversal or opposite of the underlying impulses. For example, the client who fears being rejected by other people might be asked to play the role of a hermit or recluse who could care less how others perceive and accept him.

EXAGGERATION: When the client makes a significant gesture or statement in a casual, feeble, or undeveloped manner, indicating that he is not aware of its importance, he is asked to repeat again and again with amplified movement, loudness, and/or emphasis. This facilitates the client's achieving a better contact with himself and putting more of his self into integrative communication.

MAY I FEED YOU A SENTENCE?: As the counselor-therapist attends to the verbal and nonverbal communications of the client he will decipher significant messages which are implied but apparently not in the awareness of the client. The therapist proposes a sentence for the client "to try on for size" and then to repeat it to several other persons. Although interpretation is unavoidably present, the primary objective is to enable the client to experience more of himself through active participation. A spontaneous development should follow if the sentence proves to be an accurately relevant one.

Stay-With-It

Sooner or later in the counseling process, the client hits on a feeling, mood, or state of mind that is unpleasant and he prefers to run from rather than encountering it. Instead of making it easy for the client to avoid the unpleasant situation, the counselor-therapist encourages him to "stay-with-it." If the client is able to be fully aware and to experience the painful moment, he will advance in the maturation process. Healing and growing *and* pain/suffering are bedfellows in human existence.

Directed Awareness

A basic goal of therapy, from the Gestalt view, is the reintegration of attention and awareness (Enright, 1970). Throughout the therapy process the counselor-therapist watches for splits in attention and awareness, in terms of the client's sensorimotor functioning. The therapist looks for evidence that the focus of the client's organismic attention lies outside of his awareness. The client may be aware of talking about his problem, and be totally unaware of sensorily registering and motorically doing something else — gazing at the wall, smiling, wringing the hands, etc. The "unconscious" activities may or may not be congruent with the client's verbal behavior. When an incongruence between the verbal content and the out-of-awareness behaviors is evident, it is the task of the counselor-therapist to draw these other sensorimotor activities into the client's awareness. The client can be helped to integrate his organismic attention and his awareness more appropriately by asking him what he is doing, seeing, or feeling rather than by trying to interpret his behavior to him.

Dreamwork

The dream is an existential-phenomenological message revealing the person to himself. In a very real sense the individual *is* his dream. But from another perspective, every image in a dream represents an alienated, disowned, discordant, and projected part of the self of the dreamer. Therefore, as Fritz Perls has observed, the dream is the royal road to integration.

An experiential rather than an analytical approach to dreams is required. In Gestalt dreamwork, the client first tells his dream and then plays the part of the various images, be they persons, animals, or objects. By re-experiencing and retelling the dream in the present tense — reliving the dream in the now — from the standpoint of each image, the client can begin to reclaim and integrate the alienated, disowned, and discordant parts of his personality. Interpretation, if any, of the dream is left to the client. The counselor-therapist assists by a) suggesting the order in which the images might be contacted-played, usually from the less to the more vivid ones, b) helping the client deal with avoidance and resistance in playing the disowned parts, and c) suggesting when the client might relate the images and feelings of the dream to his current situation (Enright, 1970).

The dialogue game can be used to facilitate the integration of the discordant personality parts revealed in the dream. Sometimes it may be desirable to use an empty chair in which the client changes his seat as he dialogues/interacts with a disowned part of himself as represented by a dream image.

Jungian Contributions

The Technique of Active Imagination

Much of an individual's psychic life lies outside of the realm of consciousness. The unconscious or out-of-awareness elements play a significant role in the organization of the individual's behavior patterns, and have the potential for a greater positive influence if given objective expression. One means of tapping the unconscious resources is the use of *active imagination.* By active imagination we mean the active, purposeful creation or development of a psychological image or theme.

As Jung (e.g., 1968) has suggested, unconscious images have a life of their own and can emerge according to their own logic through a series of symbolic events during the awakened state just as dreams do in the state of sleep. If the individual begins to concentrate on a particular inner image and does not interrupt the natural flow of events, the unconscious will produce a series of images which make a complete story. The unfolding of the unconscious drama can be facilitated by the use of various media: drawing, painting, writing, modeling with clay, dancing, acting, sculpturing, weaving/sewing, playing a musical instrument. The basic idea is for the client to be *with* himself and allow a theme to emerge and develop spontaneously to permit the unconscious part of the personality to communicate uninhibited with the conscious domain.

This expressive form of auto-therapy should be considered as an adjunct to other therapeutic modes. Active imagination can be used either as an in-session method or as an outside assignment or both. This technique enables the client to a) objectify his unconscious life, b) discover more fully who he really is, c) clarify his values, feelings, attitudes, and meanings, d) experience himself more spontaneously and creatively, e) quicken his psychological maturation process, and f) achieve better integration and balance in his personality functioning.

Psychoanalytic Contributions

Free Association

Clients enter the counseling-therapy room in various psychological states. Some clients arrive in fair control of their thoughts and feelings and are ready to state their concern, establish a counseling goal, and begin working toward behavior change. Others enter therapy confused, incoherent, and mentally-emotionally fatigued. Free association is hard to beat as a preliminary therapeutic procedure with the latter client situation. This method consists essentially of providing an emotionally permissive atmosphere in which the client is encouraged to utter whatever comes to mind — a sharing or reporting of his feelings, sensations, memories, experiences, and associations — with no concern with logic, order, system, or any form of conscious control (e.g., Alexander, 1963; Fine, 1973). Whether the client sits or reclines will vary with the presenting situation. Normally, the seated position is desirable, but in cases where the client is intensely befuddled, the reclining position can be more facilitative. Regardless of client position, the counselor-therapist sits beside or in front of the client (some therapists prefer to sit behind the client) and listens, encourages, clarifies, summarizes, and makes interpretive comments whenever appropriate.

When/if the therapist senses that the client is ready for a more active form of therapy or that a variant insight approach would be more efficacious, other therapeutic modes should be introduced.

(Perhaps it's worth observing that the nondirective or client-centered approach to counseling and psychotherapy follows a modified form of free association; the client is encouraged to talk about whatever he wishes, beginning wherever he likes, with the counselor encouraging him to follow certain affective avenues by reinforcing selected client expressions with approving nonverbal behaviors and reflective statements.)

Rational-Emotive Contributions

Didactic Therapy

From time to time the counselor-therapist encounters a client who leads a self-defeating life due to irrational philosophic assumptions and absolutistic beliefs about himself, about others, and about the world. With such a client, the therapist assumes an active, directive teaching role in which the client is "re-educated" to live rationally and realistically. The counselor-therapist engages the client in a Socratic-type dialogue and challenges the client's magical, illogical, irrational approach to life. The therapist uses logic and reason, suggestion, persuasion, confrontation, cajoling, contradiction, disputation, assigned reading, and prescription of behavior to enable the client a) to see what his irrational philosophies are, b) to understand how these illogical beliefs and attitudes produced his emtionally disturbed behavior, c) to see how he is sustaining or perpetuating his disturbance by continuing to think illogically, and d) to change his thinking, feeling, and performance — his life — by replacing irrational, illogical attitudes and ideas with rational, logical ones (Ellis, 1973a, 1973b). The counselor-therapist must be careful not to impose his own beliefs and philosophic assumptions on the client in the process.

Reality Therapy Contributions

Teaching Morality and Responsibility

The basic premise of reality therapy is that the client's problems stem from his inability to comprehend and apply values and moral principles in daily life so as to fulfill responsibly his basic needs of love and self-worth (Glasser, 1965; Glasser & Zunin, 1973). Although the client must face the fact of reality that he is responsible for his behavior and its modification, the counselor-therapist assumes the responsibility of teaching the client how to behave morally and responsibly in fulfilling his psychological needs.

Among the principles that characterize the teaching process the following ones are keystones: 1) the client is asked to evaluate his behavior as to whether it is responsible, and thereby good for him and others in his society; 2) the client and therapist work together to make specific, realistic plans to change failure/irresponsible behavior to success/responsible behavior, with the details of the plans stated in a written contract; 3) the client is helped to make a personal commitment to carry out the plan for behavior change in accordance with his value judgment; and 4) no excuses will be accepted for not fulfilling the commitment.

Teaching methods include "'pinning down" (requiring specificity in expressions and decision making), constructive arguing, humor, confrontations, verbal shock therapy, and *in vivo* practice of desired behavior. This therapeutic strategy is particularly appropriate for use with adolescents. It bears repeating that the teaching-therapy happens in a personal, warm, honest, and caring atmosphere where client and therapist are mutually open and involved.

Religious Contributions

Bibliotherapy

The use of literature to help individuals with personal concerns antedates by centuries the existence of formalized counseling and psychotherapy. Bibliotherapy, though found as an auxiliary method in most contemporary psychotherapies, has its historical roots in the Jewish and Christian communities. Rabbis, priests, and pastors for three millennia have directed their communicants to the Hebraic-Christian scriptures and other religious literature for information, guidance, comfort, encouragement, and spiritual-mental support and restoration. Perhaps no other literary resource has had therapeutic transport equal to that of the Book of Psalms, which covers the gamut of human emotions and experiences.

At the risk of being trite, there are scores of books and pamphlets which can be employed as excellent supplements to the counseling process. Biographies can be used as a form of symbolic social modeling to enable clients to see how other individuals coped with the same problems which they themselves have. Inspirational literature can be a source of nurture and motivation to the despondent and melancholy client. Some bibliotherapeutic literature, e.g., the Public Affairs pamphlets and the SRA Life-Adjustment Booklets, is designed specifically to help the "layperson" to cope with a variety of human concerns. In some cases, the counseling-therapy process will be more meaningful to the client if he is directed to a book that describes the particular type of therapy which he is encountering (e.g., a client in transactional analytic counseling-therapy certainly would want to read either *I'm OK — You're OK, What Do You Say After You Say Hello?* or *Born to Win*).

Brammer and Shostrom (1968) have drawn up a set of principles to guide the use of bibliotherapy. First, the counselor-therapist must possess a knowledge of the books which he recommends. Familiarity with the books enables the counselor to refer a client to the appropriate book in terms of topic or content, age range, experience, and language or reading level. Second, reading material should be suggested rather than prescribed, and the counselor-therapist should give evidence that he endorses with confidence the ideas in the material. Third, the reading should be timed and the suggestion made when the therapist senses that the client a) will not perceive that his problem is being considered as of minor importance, b) will not interpret the literature to be a substitute for the counseling process proper, c) will not judge the counselor to be incompetent to help him, and d) is in a period of low resistance. Fourth, discussion should follow the client's reading in order to ascertain the effect of the reading, to correct any distortions and misunderstandings, and to make a realistic evaluation of the ideas. Fifth, lists of suggested readings, preferably with annotations, and selected books and pamphlets can be placed in the waiting room for client self-referral. Finally, reading should be suggested or "assigned" in small amounts, since too much material might discourage or distract the client.

Trait-Factor and Clinical Contributions

Psychological Testing

Psychological assessment is particularly appropriate as a counseling technique with clients who present educational and vocational concerns, but the use of tests need not be limited to these two areas.

Traditionally, psychological tests have been used to obtain diagnostic information. Results of diagnostic psychological assessment either reinforce or counter the counselor-therapist's understanding of the client and his situation and thus influence the therapeutic strategy. In addition to the diagnostic function, tests can provide the client a) an opportunity for gaining a better self-understanding in terms of his strengths and deficiencies; b) a reality-testing medium for checking the accuracy of his perceptions of his abilities and traits, and the reasonableness of the goals which he has set or will set for himself; c) a stimulus to explore his motivations and feelings as they relate to possible endeavors and engagements; d) an opportunity for further exploration and discovery of his aptitudes, achievements, interests, values, and attitudes; and e) a basis for judging the probabilities of success in specific areas of interest (Bordin, 1968).

The following are some basic guidelines for using psychological tests. In the first place, the counselor-therapist must be well prepared to use various kinds of tests and feel comfortable with them. Secondly, the client should participate actively in test selection rather than the counselor prescribing it/them at will or routinely. When the counselor-therapist senses that the client is at the point where more data about himself would be helpful (the point may come at any time during the counseling process), the possibility of tests is suggested. The counselor describes the categories of tests and recommends the ones that get at the psychological characteristics with which the client is most concerned at this time. After the client has responded and reacted to each of the recommended tests, a final selection is made and arrangements are made for taking the tests. Third, the test results must be interpreted accurately and realistically to the client in clear, non-technical, and non-evaluative terms or phraseology. The counselor must be ever careful a) to remember that test results are merely a sample of client behavior at the time of the testing, b) not to isolate test results from other client data, and c) to make sure that the client knows what type of measure is being discussed and which norm group is being used. Finally, a constellation of test results is favored over the data derived from a single instrument. For example, when a college sophomore seeks help with indecision regarding the selection of a major and career objective, rather than relying solely on the *Strong Vocational Interest Blank* (measure of interests), the client might gain a much better self-understanding if he also takes the *Edwards Personal Preference Schedule* (measure of personality), the *Allport-Lindzey Study of Values* (measure of values), and the *Sequential Tests of Educational Progress* (measure of achievement).

Transactional Analytic Contributions

Structural Analysis

The fundamental technique of transactional analytic therapy is structural analysis. The client is trained to become an expert in understanding the structure and the functioning of his own personality. The human personality manifests three types of ego or psychological states which can be labeled appropriately as Parent, Adult, and Child. Each ego state is a phenomenological reality that is produced in the here and now of life by the "playback of recorded data" of past events and experiences (Harris, 1969). The *Parent* represents values, attitudes, and perceptions of external events which were introjected and/or internalized (recorded) by the individual in the early years of life. The Parent data were acquired principally from the individual's actual parents and are typically archaic relative to current living. The *Child* is the recording of the feelings the individual formed about himself and others during his first five years. These feeling-based Child data are decisions made before the individual had a vocabulary adequate to give his experience cognitive registry; therefore, the body of Child data operates at a high level of unawareness in here and now existence (and the same holds true for Parent data). The *Adult* ego state refers to the mental recording of data gathered from the Parent, the Child, and the exploration of reality, and computed for accuracy and proper fit. Thus, reality-oriented Adult data consist of a) updated and validated Parent data, b) updated reality data, and c) updated, appropriate Child data.

Through a more detailed structural analysis, the client discovers additional truth about his ego states. His Parent can exhibit itself either as a Nurturing Parent or as a Controlling Parent. Similarly, the Child ego state manifests itself at times as a free, self-expressive Natural Child, at other times as a well-behaved Adapted Child, and sometimes as a misbehaved Rebellious Child. Further structural analysis may disclose that the client is unable to function effectively as a balanced organism due to either a) a Parent-contaminated Adult*, or b) a Child-contaminated Adult, or c) a Parent and Child-contaminated Adult, or d) a Parent-contaminated Adult with an excluded Child**, or e) a Child-contaminated Adult with an excluded Parent, or f) a constant Parent with an excluded Adult, or g) a constant Child with an excluded Adult, or h) a constant Adult with an excluded Parent and Child.

The primary objective of structural analysis is to enable the client to be aware of his ego states and to identify the particular ego state from which he is functioning at any given time in his social intercourse.

Transactional Analysis

The central process or technique in transactional analytic therapy is the analysis of transactions. If structural analysis can be conceived as comprehension of the fundamental anatomy of personality, then transactional analysis may be perceived as the investigation of the basic dynamics of personality functioning. Just as the ego state is the unit of structural analysis, the transaction is the unit of transactional analysis.

Every communication between two persons may be viewed as a transaction. A completed transaction consists of a transactional stimulus followed by a transactional response. The voice on either end of the transaction may be from the Parent, the Adult, or the Child. As long as the transactional stimulus and the transactional response are complementary or parallel vectors, communication between two persons can continue indefinitely. *Complementary transactions* are the basis of "good" interpersonal relationships. Whenever the stimulus emitted by the ego state of the sender "hooks" an ego state in the other person and evokes a response which is nonparallel with the transactional stimulus, a *crossed transaction* results. Uncomplementary or crossed transactions lead to interruptions and breakdowns in communication and are characteristic of "bad" interpersonal relationships. In a third form of transaction, the *ulterior transaction*, the stimulus operates at two levels — the overt-social and the covert-psychological. The be-

* Contamination is the behavioral phenomenon observed when the boundaries between two ego states overlap and the content of one interferes with the functioning of the other.
** Exclusion exists when an entire ego state is denied by its possessor and not allowed direct and recognized expression in his feelings and behavior.

havioral outcome of an ulterior transaction is determined at the psychological level, and this manner of interacting is at the heart of all games. The three basic forms of transactions are illustrated in Figure 5.

A significant part of transactional analysis is the identification of the types of experiences an individual uses to structure time and gain strokes/recognition. Transactional experiences or social interactions include withdrawal, rituals, activities, pastimes, games, and intimacy.

Transactional analysis seeks to enable the client to monitor effectively his transactions — to be aware of the ego states from which transactions emanate and of the ego states to which the transactions are directed, and to communicate smoothly by having the capacity to cathect the appropriate ego states in sequential interactions so as to sustain complementarity of transactional stimuli and responses.

Script Analysis

Each person has a life plan or script. The script is essentially an "unconscious" decision that was made at an early age as to how life should be lived. Thus, the script is feeling-oriented and centered in the Child ego state.

Central to script analysis is *positional analysis,* which is concerned with helping the client to decipher his basic position in life. All human relationships are founded upon the "I - Others" polarity. Furthermore, the specific nature or character of any interpersonal relationship is determined by a particular combination of the polarity "OK - NOT OK" (I am/you are good, accepted, liked, approved, respected, capable, desirable, loved, appreciated, worthy of recognition *versus* I am/you are bad, rejected, disliked, disapproved, despised, inadequate, undesirable, unloved, unappreciated, unworthy of recognition). The life position plays a major role in determining the script the person will pursue throughout life. The four possible life positions are:

1. I'M NOT OK — YOU'RE OK
2. I'M NOT OK — YOU'RE NOT OK
3. I'M OK — YOU'RE NOT OK
4. I'M OK — YOU'RE OK

Only the fourth position, I'M OK — YOU'RE OK, is truly wholesome. An individual who seeks counseling-therapy suffers from one of the first three positions. Each of the three positions is based totally on stroking (nurture and positive reinforcement) and non-

FIGURE 5

Diagrams of Complementary, Crossed, and Ulterior Transactions

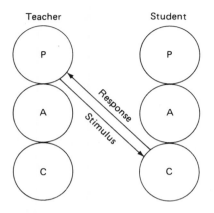

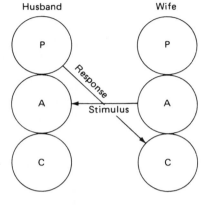

(A) Complementary Transaction

Teacher: John, your project should be completed no later than Friday.

Student: O.K., Mr. Peterson.

(B) Crossed Transaction

Wife: What would you like for dinner?

Husband: Here goes the indecisive one again.

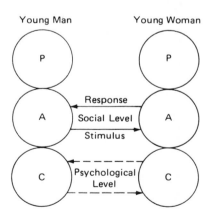

(C) Ulterior Transaction

Young Man: Let's go to my apartment and enjoy some good music.

Young Woman: Great! I love good music.

stroking (lack of nurture and positive reinforcement). Harris (1969) postulates that:

> The I'M NOT OK — YOU RE OK is the first tentative decision based on the experiences of the first year of life. By the end of the second year it is either confirmed and settled or it gives way to position 2 or 3. [see above] . . . Once finalized, the child stays in his chosen position and it governs everything he does. It stays with him the rest of his life, unless he later consciously changes it to the fourth position. [p. 43]

Since the client has been unable through the process of normal growth and development to achieve the position I'M OK — YOU'RE OK (a conscious, verbal decision made about self and others that is reached by the data-gathering and data-processing functions of the Adult ego state), this becomes a process-goal of therapy.

The client's *racket* is also examined in script analysis. The racket represents the feelings which an individual collects to justify major actions in his life script. Anger, guilt, hostility, and despair are illustrative of the feelings which the client might be interested in experiencing, saving up, and trading-in for strokes or recognition.

Finally, the *games* which the client plays to maintain his racket and to advance his life script are analyzed. In essence a game consists of an orderly series of complementary transactions which are marked by an ulterior motive and result in an emotional payoff — a neurotic means of getting what one wants or needs.

The objective of script analysis is to give the client an awareness of how he acquired the script, how he goes about justifying his script action, and how he can rewrite his script and enjoy a racket-free, game-free approach to life.

Termination

The counseling-therapy process is initiated with the awareness that it will be a temporary involvement. Some therapeutic encounters endure for only a single session while other counselor-client interactions continue for weeks, months, and, in some cases, for years. But when the counselor-therapist and client no longer see each other for the express purpose of working toward behavior modification, the counseling-therapy process is terminated. The following discussion focuses on a number of variables that bear upon the termination of counseling-therapy.

A Constant Issue

Termination should be a central issue in the counseling-therapy process from the very beginning. Since the client is respected as an essentially free being having the right to be self-determining and self-directing, he is encouraged as early as possible in the therapeutic encounter to assume responsibility for deciding to continue counseling-therapy. Although the counselor-therapist tries at all times to provide the conditions necessary and sufficient for behavior change, it must be the prerogative of the client to judge whether he is getting enough from therapy to warrant continuing with it. The client cannot reasonably terminate without first evaluating his progress toward achieving his goal. We would expect the client who is aware of making substantial progress toward his objective to be motivated adequately to continue the process. Thus, the entire course of counseling-therapy can be enhanced when termination is a viable issue from the initial interview and the client is fully aware that the decision is principally his.

Premature Termination

Encouraging the client to assume the basic responsibility for deciding to continue therapy does not mean that the counselor accepts unchallenged the client's desire to terminate prematurely and follow an easy-out path. There are times when the client would prefer to depart counseling-therapy rather than come to grips with himself and make the necessary changes in his behavior. The perceptive therapist detects and confronts the client's resistance and adjunct avoidance behaviors. Becoming aware of the unreasonable and superficial basis for desiring termination and experiencing support and encouragement from the counselor, the client is likely to continue to work toward his counseling goal.

Sooner or later every counselor-therapist encounters his first client who tells him, either with words or by not showing for the next appointment, that the counselor and the counseling process are of no help to him. Rather than viewing this premature termination as a challenge to his professional competency, the counselor-therapist would do well to accept it as a fact of reality that he cannot expect to be effective with all clients. Whenever possible, the counselor should discuss the issue openly with the client and express his true feelings, including his disappointment in not being able to work with the client until the goal was attained. Too, the counselor should express in some form the idea that he yet respects the client and is glad the client was able to verbalize his decision and feelings.

Occasionally the counseling process is terminated before the objectives of the encounter have been fulfilled due to external events in the life of the counselor, such as moving and the closing of an office or agency. If these events are anticipated, the client can be prepared for the termination by being informed early in the process. But when the occurrences arise unexpectedly, efforts must be made to assist the client with making new adjustments. If the counselor and client have formed a strong relationship, the counselor must be concerned with client feelings which are generated by the news of the soon-to-be-broken relationship. The client is likely to feel that he has been betrayed by a trusted friend. Feelings of hurt, anger, fear, and resentment can emerge as the client reflects on how he divulged confidential material to one who is now "walking out" on him. An honest, open sharing of the feelings of both the client and the counselor-therapist is necessary. If another counselor is desired by the client, the departing counselor-therapist should do all he can to assist with the referral and transitional procedures.

Fulfilled Counseling Goals

Ideally, the counseling-therapy process is concluded only after the specified goals for the process have been successfully met. One process criterion discussed eralier in this chapter requires that it must be possible to observe to what extent the client achieves his personally desired and stated goal(s). Therefore, after the appropriate therapeutic methods have been applied to the client's situation, within the parameters of a facilitative relationship, so as to effect the desired change in his life style or behavior, then termination of therapy is appropriate.

Both the client and the therapist must be able to observe change, in terms of the desired outcome. The change must not be observable only in the therapy room, but be substantiated as well *in vivo*. For example, if a client's goal for counseling is to be able to write exams without excessive anxiety, it is unreasonable to think of terminating therapy until he can write exams *in vivo* without excessive anxiety.

Thus, when the client stands assured that he has satisfied his counseling objective and is able to corroborate his self-report with validating evidence from reality-testing, the counseling process is terminated.

Goodbye

Terminating a strong counseling relationship generates mixed emotions in both the client and the counselor-therapist. Both are happy that progress has been made and the client no longer needs the assistance of the therapist. Both also experience sadness because they have become friends — fellow human beings who have encountered one another in real life — and now must discontinue the relationship. Both are richer because of the experience and feel it would be nice to meet again next week but think it far better not to do so. So, they shake hands, or perhaps embrace, smile affectionately, and say a mutual "Goodbye." As the client walks away, he senses deep in his heart that he has found a person who not only cares for him but has touched his life in a healing, strengthening way. He knows that the "door is always open" and he can return for additional healing or help if the need arises in the future. And as the counselor-therapist leans back in his chair or looks reflectively out his window, he too feels deep within himself that he has helped to make a life a bit more meaningful for another person and that person in turn has made life a bit fuller for him.

4

....

Application

This chapter presents two cases in outline form to illustrate how integrative counseling and psychotherapy theory may be applied to specific counseling-therapy situations. The case presentations are limited to the two because, in the first place, space prohibits the inclusion of a larger number of cases and, secondly, we speculate that the gain to the reader would be insignificantly greater from reading a score of cases rather than a dyad of illustrative ones.

The cases presented are based on real client situations in which the author was involved as the counselor-therapist. The names of the clients and other demographic variables surrounding the cases have been modified to preserve the privacy of the individuals.

The establishment and maintenance of a client-counselor relationship of the nature delineated in Chapter 3 is to be assumed by the reader for each of the cases. Following a brief introductory description of the client-problem situation, an analysis is made of the presenting problem. After the disturbing behavior has been carefully analyzed, a goal or a series of goals to work toward in the counseling-therapy process is formulated. Behavioral analysis and the statement of counseling objectives are followed by the selection and application of the therapeutic methods deemed appropriate for the particular client-problem situation. The methods may be applied either singly, in tandem, or sequentially to effect the desired change in client behavior.

Cindy

Behavioral Analysis

Cindy, a twenty-two year old graduate student, complained that life held no meaning for her. She had recently taken the Bachelor's degree with majors in psychology and sociology and entered graduate school primarily to be near her boyfriend of better than four years standing, but, also, because there seemed to be nothing else that she could do. The romance had now turned sour and graduate study, like all the rest of her current experiences, was perceived as an irrelevant and meaningless "bag of garbage." Cindy was cynical and pessimistic toward her world and other people and traced the negative attitudes to her disappointment and disillusionment with love. She sensed that during the last two or three years she had become progressively more of a solitary figure with fewer and fewer friends. Cindy stated that she had no goal in life except maybe the longing for an intimate relationship in which she and a man could give and receive mutual love, but she was so afraid that "it will never happen."

Preliminary Analysis of the Problem Situation

Cindy's inability to find a concrete goal in life and to establish a satisfying relationship with a male partner appeared to be at the heart of her situation. Her frustrated efforts to discover purpose and meaning in life resulted in Cindy's blaming the environment for her undesirable predicament. The client was highly critical of the "social system," wanted to have nothing to do with its materialistic snatchgrabbing, and was withdrawing from it into her own private and insular world. Cindy had little or no interest in having female friends, and her dreams were wrapped up in the hope of becoming permanently involved with a male lover. She believed that if the right man should come along all her problems would be solved. But since she was sure that the right man would never enter her life, Cindy was resigning herself to a pessimistic, meaningless existence.

Clarification of the Problem Situation

As the analysis progressed, it became quite clear that Cindy for more than four years had had no plans other than marrying her lately-lost lover. She had "placed all her eggs in one basket" and lost. The client felt exploited, jilted, abandoned, that something must be wrong with her, and that she was a personal failure. Although she had no real interest in her study of graduate psychology, Cindy sensed that she must continue with it since she was financially dependent on her father, and *the* condition for support was working toward an advanced degree. Thus, the immediate problem situation appeared to have been precipitated by aborted — apparently one-sided — plans for marriage. The client was then left dangling without a goal in life and faced with the need to survive financially but in terms of the father's prescribed contingencies of reinforcement. Cindy, harboring feelings of hurt, anger, resentment, and helplessness, found herself retreating from life.

Developmental Analysis

Cindy and her two-years-younger sister grew up in a socially competitive subdivision of a large metropolitan area. The father, a well-to-do businessman, was viewed by Cindy as being an intelligent, clever, and smooth-talking entrepreneur but an authoritarian husband and father. Cindy perceived her mother to be intellectually simple and emotionally passive. The parents never seemed to love and be happy with one another; they were always too concerned with keeping up with or getting ahead of the neighbors. According to Cindy, the family environment had always been affectively impoverished and very neurotic. The client often fantasized of being married and having a home life different from that of her parents. Cindy expressed feelings of hostility toward her parents, especially the father. She had experienced much punishment but very little love from her father.

Cindy's academic performance was quite commendable throughout her educational history. She "didn't have to work very hard at all" to get the marks, mostly A's and B's, in contrast to her sister who had to struggle for a B. However, school never meant very much to Cindy since so many of the courses lacked relevance.

The client had done nothing of an occupational nature except merchandising a few items furnished by her father. She sensed no need to do anything because her father had the means to provide for her and would always come through. Even though hostile toward her father and resentful for having to be dependent on him, Cindy seemed to like the idea of *not* planning for a career or occupation. In fact, she verbalized her abhorrence of making plans for an occupation in which she could possibly "get trapped." Cindy thought it might be nice to become a housewife who was free to dabble in arts and crafts.

From the psychosexual perspective, the client was quite enamored with her pretty face and slender body. She claimed superiority to her sister in these categories as well as in the intellectual area. Quite noticeable was a much underdeveloped bustline in the client, and Cindy indicated in a circuitous manner that she was envious of her sister's larger breasts. The client remarked that both she and her sister had cute "baby faces."

Analysis of the Existential Status and Self-Control

This aspect of the analysis disclosed a number of factors. As indicated in the introductory description of the case, the client was cynical, pessimistic, and found no real meaning in her life experiences. Cindy stated that the four plus years spent with the boyfriend stymied her life by isolating her from forming a circle of friendships and keeping her emotionally dependent. A woman biologically and chronologically, Cindy viewed herself as a child emotionally and socially. Cindy acknowledged that she was starved from the lack of affection and love, and it was apparent that she sought to achieve recognition, particularly from males, through her highly seductive modes of dress and body movements. The client considered herself a "loner," and tended to avoid as much as possible all older individuals except interesting males; she spent very little time with other females. Cindy was skeptical of both the present and the future.

Analysis of the Environmental Press

The client saw herself standing essentially alone in an undesirable situation. She had been abandoned by a supposed lover and left amidst a meaningless course of graduate studies. Regardless of how unpalatable the studies might be, she felt that she must continue them in order to save face with her friends, her parents, and her professors and to maintain financial sustenance from her father. Cindy felt trapped and saw no option other than sticking with her situation. It was obvious that the values and expectations of others were having a much greater influence on Cindy's life than were her own.

Counseling-Therapy Goals

Cindy and the counselor agreed on three principal goals for the counseling-therapy encounter. The goals were stated in Cindy's terms as follows:

1. To find some goal or purpose in life so as to have something concrete to work toward and to give meaning to life.

2. To be less critical of other people.
3. To make new friends and to become more actively involved with people, especially fellow students, rather than withdrawing from them.

Counseling-Therapy Methods

Three modes of therapy were used to assist Cindy with the achievement of her objectives. The methods consisted of Adlerian-type life style analysis (which was in certain aspects a particularized extension of the behavioral analysis), logotherapy, and assertive training.

The behavioral analysis suggested that the family background was making a definite contribution to the present situation of the client. Too, Cindy's goals for counseling indicated that she wished to develop a more wholesome social interest. Thus, life style analysis seemed most appropriate as the initial therapeutic method. A basic objective of the life style analysis was to ascertain, and facilitate insight into, the basic mistakes which Cindy had made in the past that were interfering with her current efforts towards the fulfillment of life tasks. An investigation of the family constellation revealed that Cindy had assumed psychological superiority to all other members of the family, including her dominant father. The client tended to see herself as pretty, intelligent, and desirable, while others in the family were described as being either unshapely, lazy, intellectually simple, neurotic, passive, snobbish, or greedy. Cindy's early recollections centered on playing alone with her dolls and relating to her classmates with aggressive, hostile behaviors. She speculated that the childhood hostility stemmed from the frustration caused by speech difficulties.

The overall analysis of the life style indicated that Cindy had formed a number of unrealistic perceptions of self and her social world. First, an exaggerated view of her physical and intellectual attributes was erected to compensate for a basic feeling of personal inferiority. This was at the base of her haughty and critical attitudes toward other people. Secondly, Cindy decided early in life that there was no need to work hard nor to plan for a vocation because her father was well-off financially and she would ever be amply supplied with the necessities of life; therefore, no goal in life. Thirdly, due to her own unhappiness and insecurity and the perceived marital unhappiness of her parents, Cindy formed a fairytale concept of love and marriage in which some strong and caring man would eventually enter her life, they would fall deeply in love and marry, and then life would be full and beautiful. Living with this fanciful expectation and counting on the father's financial backing constituted the essence of Cindy's "goal" in life when therapy was begun. Fourthly, not having received love from her parents and having failed up to now to experience a mutual and lasting love relationship with a man were causing Cindy to believe that she was unlovable and that she was destined to live apart from real love. Finally, Cindy had learned that she could partially meet her needs for love, affection, and attention through seductive dress and body language. The analysis enabled the client to see the foundation of her ineffective and self-defeating style of living.

In the next phase of therapy the counselor engaged Cindy in logotherapeutic dialogue to explore the meanings of life, love, marriage, and work. The general aim was to help the client to become fully aware that she was no longer, nor should want to be, "Daddy's dependent and irresponsible little girl" but, as a *free* and *responsible adult*, to begin to formulate a mature, realistic philosophy/style of living to replace the superficial and erroneous decisions she had previously drawn. Through the dialogue, Cindy began to realize how egocentric her behaviors had been, how passively dependent she really was, just how idyllic and impractical were her views of love and marriage, how and why she had avoided making essential life decisions, and the methods she was using to manipulate other people. In order to cultivate social interest or feelings, Cindy a) de-reflected feelings about herself and critical thoughts about others by focusing on the good qualities in these heretofore put-down people, and b) sought ways to be helpful to others. A discussion of the meaning and value of creative work resulted in Cindy's discovering that a helping profession such as teaching or counseling could be a rewarding mission in life. With this new discovery, she became enthused with the idea of becoming a professional helper and her graduate program in psychology began to be considered a significant means to a desirable end. It was also personally rewarding to Cindy to envision her establishing financial independence of her father since much of her hostility toward him arose from resenting her sustained dependency on her father.

The next step in the therapy process involved the use of assertive training to enable Cindy to overcome her shyness and timidity and to develop courage and confidence to meet new people and establish some friendships. The counselor and Cindy rehearsed behaviors such as initiating conversations, participating actively in social events, and entertaining a few people in her apartment. These behaviors were subsequently practiced in the actual environment. Since Cindy discovered in therapy that the past boyfriend was used as a ready excuse for not having to make new friends, both the client and counselor sensed the wisdom in her having as large a circle of friends as possible, male and female, and *not* to become attached to one individual.

The counseling-therapy process was terminated after nine sessions. It was mutually perceived by client and counselor-therapist that the goals had been sufficiently realized. Cindy yet had a long way to go with making friends, but she was doing well at the task. Cindy dropped in from time to time after the termination to share a new discovery or to discuss a personal concern. Perhaps the greatest accomplishments in the entire encounter were Cindy's discovering what love really is, finding a purpose in living, and learning how to stand on her own two feet as a self-directing and decisive person.

Kent

Behavioral Analysis

Kent was a Ph.D. chemical engineer in his late twenties, single, and employed by a pharmaceutical firm. He came to the counselor-therapist on a self-referral basis.

The client's initial complaint was that he was having extreme difficulty in relating to people. Kent expressed that he felt as if he were "divided" within himself regarding his attitudes toward others. On the one hand, he liked and wanted to be near people, but, on the other hand, he preferred to get away from people and hide himself in his lonely apartment. Kent verbalized, "It seems as if I like and dislike people at the same time."

Near the mid-point of the first session the client stared silently into space for a long duration. At length the counselor asked, "Kent, what are you seeing right now?" The client responded with, "All the problems in my life." The counselor-therapist then suggested that Kent might begin to talk about some of the things that were bothering him. The client said that he wanted to but it was very difficult. The therapist sensed that the content was very painful to the client and that he was afraid to disclose it. The client stated that this was the situation. The counselor-therapist assured the client that he would be respected and unjudged regardless of what the concern might be. At that juncture the client seemed to retreat psychologically from the counselor. This phenomenon was verbalized to the client. The client shared that it was necessary for him to withdraw deep within in order to say what he had to get out. Kent then placed his face in his hands, rested his elbows on his knees, looked despairingly at the floor, and said, "I'm a homosexual."

Preliminary Analysis of the Problem Situation

Reduced to the simplest terms, the client was a homosexual who aspired to be a heterosexual. In his feelings and desires, Kent was strongly attracted to males. But, intellectually and philosophically, he preferred heterosexuality. Thus, Kent's ideal heterosexual self was in constant conflict with his practical or actual homosexual self.

The client reported that considerable guilt surrounded his behaviors. His sexual desires toward males were uncontrollable but his values kept reminding him that the desires were bad or wrong. Kent also realized that the larger segment of society would disapprove of his behavior and this necessitated his being ever on guard to conceal his essential self from the public. He speculated how much more easy and pleasant life would be if he were a practicing heterosexual.

Disconcerting to the client was the feeling that he had to assume always a passive and secondary role in life. He perceived this to be true for all his interpersonal, social, and work relationships. For example, Kent sensed that during professional meetings at his firm his ideas were typically sloughed off by his colleagues and he was forced to take a back-seat position to the more aggressive members of the staff.

Clarification of the Problem Situation

The problem was defined more clearly when the client disclosed that he needed very much to share reciprocal love with emotionally and physically strong males who were several years his senior. Although there were a number of men who served as such stimuli to the client, his needs remained basically unmet due to either the nonresponsiveness of these males or the client's fear of letting them gain knowledge of his interests. The client's principal need, he claimed, was for affection communicated through the medium of an embrace. He stated that total sexual involvement became ugly and repulsive. In fact, part of the immediate concern of the client was the one responsive male in his world who desired full involvement. The client did not want to lose the affection and friendship of the partner, but he wished to avoid the complete sexual act.

While the client had an intellectual interest in relating interpersonally to women, he found them to be an averse stimulus, especially large and/or possessive women. Kent went so far as to say that he would like eventually to be married to a woman but such a relationship was utterly impossible given his current psychological disposition toward women. He postulated that a platonic love relationship would probably be his closest approximation of intimacy ever with a woman.

Central to Kent's problem were his ambivalent attraction to males and his aversion toward women. He was unable to experience persons of either sex enjoyably and meaningfully. This frustration permeated the entirety of the client's environment and affected all his movements, and, when left to his own resources to resolve the situation, he felt helpless and hopeless.

Developmental Analysis

Kent had no brothers and one sister who was two years older than he. He and the sister were "never very close" to each other, and the sister related to Kent as an "older brother" after they reached adolescence. The father was a hard-working and skilled craftsman. He was very stern and disciplined and seldom played with his son. Kent remembered how as a little boy he longed for his father to hug him, to pick him up and jostle him playfully, but it never happened. The father's physical strength and perfectionistic tendencies caused Kent to feel inferior and inadequate before his father. The father was never cruel but was cold, rigid, and aloof. It was the mother in whom Kent confided in his developmental years. She was warm and understanding but was too possessive and overprotective. The family atmosphere was marked by fundamentalistic religious beliefs and values, individual autonomy, and very little open demonstration of love and affection. The family had relatively few friends, and, since the parents were immigrants, no relatives were near enough to exchange visits.

Kent recalled not wanting his mother and sister, particularly the sister, to touch him physically. He preferred the touch of the father but didn't get it. Kent reported the trauma he experienced as a child when he was exploring the anatomical structure of a little girl whose mother discovered them, glowered at him, and called him an animal. Equally traumatic was the time he saw his mother partially nude and wearing a bloody sanitary napkin. The client began at an early age, around six or seven, to fantasize his touching the genitals of other boys. He also remembered the sensation he felt when he and his father went to the gymnasium and he saw the men with large penises in the shower. The client recounted how he would blush in early adolescence when he would hear his classmates talk about "queers." He realized then his strong latent homosexuality but it wasn't until around sixteen that he experienced his first overt act with a middle aged man. The desire for men had persisted ever since. There were times when Kent had substantial interest in females but shied away because he felt sexually inadequate; he was afraid even to kiss a woman. The client related that he once dated a girl for a number of years. Worthy of mention is the fact that sex was a taboo topic in the client's family.

The client's medical record indicated that he was physically normal and had no type of organic defect that would incapacitate him in any way.

The client had an excellent academic record as witnessed to by his Ph.D. in chemical engineering. However, Kent had a very poor social life throughout his educational history. He had taken an intellectual and analytical approach to everything and had avoided social involvement and recreational activities, especially competitive games. He felt physically inferior to both aggressive males and females.

Occupationally, the client questioned his competency. He felt that he was not nearly so good as his colleagues and that he was not making progress in his profession. He perceived that his personal problems were "holding him back" in life.

Analysis of the Existential Status and Self-Control

The client was experiencing considerable loneliness and discouragement. His inability to enter bona fide interpersonal relationships and feelings of being a second-rate person were extremely self-defeating to Kent. He had a large number of superficial relationships but was really intimate with no one. The client assumed a variety of pseudosocial roles to mask his true feelings toward men and women. He feigned friendliness with women, who were actually averse to him, by a phony smile and forced politeness. In his social encounters with men, the client tended either to talk excessively or to withdraw into a passive sullenness. Kent struggled constantly with his uncontrollable feelings, and he was ever fearful that his acquaintances would gain awareness of his inner life. Also disturbing to the client was his lack of ability to be constructively assertive and reasonably aggressive in his social and professional transactions. Although Kent enjoyed retreating to the safety of his personally decorated apartment, it was there that he experienced the greatest loneliness.

Analysis of the Environmental Press

As a religious person the client was keenly aware of the values and expectations of the religious community. Kent's problematic behavior was at variance with both the values of the community and his own values. One motive for counseling-therapy was the alignment of his behavior with these commonly held values. Kent was particularly concerned that his religious beliefs would be respected in the therapy process, and he was assured that they would be.

The client verbalized how important his homosexual confidant was to him and that he feared that the counselor-therapist would ask him to sever the relationship. The counselor gave the client assurance that it was not his prerogative to make such a demand and suggested that the relationship might play a significant role in the counseling-therapy process as the client sought to change his behavior.

The counselor inquired if there were any non-threatening females in the client's world to whom he would like to relate. Kent stated that there was one and plans were made to involve her in the therapy process at the appropriate time.

Counseling-Therapy Goals

Kent decided on the following specific goals to aim for in the counseling-therapy process:

1. To overcome or reduce his aversion to women.
2. To learn how to develop close friendships with men without the sexual desires.
3. To be effectively aggressive and assertive in his interpersonal transactions, especially in his work environment.

Counseling-Therapy Methods

Three sessions were devoted to the analysis of the disturbing behavior and the formulation of objectives for the therapy process. Analysis of the client's developmental history indicated that there was a residual of unresolved feelings from events and situations which took place during his first sixteen years of life. Although the events were historical, the feelings and memories associated with them were yet very much alive. The next two sessions focused on these historical events. Using the Gestalt unfinished business technique, the client was asked to relive the situations in the present tense of here and now existence. He was not only willing but eager to do so. Kent relived scenes such as seeing his semi-nude mother wearing the bloody sanitary napkin, the angry mother who came upon him in the act of examining the sexual makeup of her daughter, fantasizing the touching of the genitals of other boys, the feelings he had when he saw the penises of the men in the shower, the hurt and embarrassment he felt when his father showed his friends (Kent's) a picture of him dressed in his mother's clothing, blushing when his schoolmates talked about queers, and his first act of overt homosexuality. Reliving this series of events increased the client's awareness of his true feelings and facilitated a deeper understanding of his behavior. He discovered that it was the crotch area of the woman that was most averse to him. The client recalled that after seeing his menstrous mother he had a frightening dream in which she was dying. Subsequently, he perceived the female genitals as being filthy, ugly, and dreadful. Kent also saw more clearly that he needed the masculine love and affection of his father in order to feel strong and secure. He began to look to other males to meet this need since his father failed to do so. The client viewed the penis as a symbol of strength and stability. Though he desired masculine intimacy apart from the sexual act, indeed became repulsed by the sexual involvement, it was difficult to achieve intimacy without being conscious of the penis. The client attributed much of his confusion to his being ignorant of sex and the human body as a youngster.

The client stated that he would like to begin working on his attitudes toward the female body. Therefore, two sessions were given to the exploration of Kent's feelings, responses, and reactions to pictures of nude and semi-nude women in magazines such as *Oui, Penthouse,* and *Playboy.* The client resisted at first on the grounds that he would feel guilty from using pornographic materials. The counselor-therapist, sensing that the client's resistance stemmed from his religious beliefs, shared that he too was a religious person but thought it possible to use the periodicals as a learning device rather than lewd objects. This made sense to the client, and we proceeded with the task. The client reacted very positively to the pictures featuring slender and non- or slightly seductive women. The counselor verbally reinforced the client's positive responses. The client reacted most negatively to the highly seductive pictures, and particularly to those showing the woman with open legs and/or in a position that invited sexual intercourse. When asked what part of the pictured body was most difficult to encounter, the client reported that it was the pubic region. He enjoyed looking at and touching the face and the breasts but wished to avoid the genital area. After a period of time the client began to feel comfortable while touching the genital region of a woman in a position suggesting intercourse. Again, the client was positively reinforced for this behavior.

Near the end of the seventh session the client reported that he and a female date had gone (during the interim between the sixth and seventh sessions) to see the play "Butterflies Are Free." An actress in the play had worn only a bra and bikini panties. The client stated that, to his own amazement, he fantasized walking onto the stage, pulling the actress' panties down, and touching her genitals. He felt really turned on by and to the young woman. The counselor proceeded to verbally reinforce the client and to give him a pat on the back. The only discouraging factor in the mind of the client was the fact that he felt afraid to kiss his date goodnight; he experienced discomfort just holding her hand, thinking that he was expected to do more than hold her hand but felt inadequate to perform.

The time seemed ripe for bringing the client's female friend more fully into the therapy process according to the tentative plans made during the behavioral analysis. The issues were discussed and the client affirmed that he was ready to make concrete *in vivo* efforts to modify his behavior with women. The counselor-therapist suggested that an attractive female co-therapist might be advisable to help with in-session objectives. The client thought it was an excellent idea *if* the co-therapist were shorter and younger than he. The person the counselor-therapist had in mind met the conditions, and plans were made to involve her in the therapy process next session.

It was mutually agreed that the client, co-therapist, and therapist would work within the confines of the value structure of each. Nothing would be done in the counseling-therapy sessions beyond what was socially acceptable. Specifically, there would be no attempts toward sexual involvement of any kind between the participants in the therapy process. Several sessions were devoted to modeling and rehearsing the specific behaviors desired by the client. For example, talking and relating to a woman in a sincere and relaxed manner, feeling comfortable while holding a woman's hand, being able to embrace and kiss a woman, and the ability and/or courage to talk to a woman about his feelings and attitudes. The therapist and co-therapist first modeled these and other behaviors for the client, followed by the client rehearsing them with the co-therapist. The client then sought to put them into practice with his female confidante in the real world. The counselor-therapists continually reinforced him for even the smallest degree of success and encouraged him to continue his efforts. When he reported failure, the ineffective behaviors were rehearsed again and again, sometimes with modification, until the client felt courageous enough to try them once more *in vivo*. After nine sessions the client was able to function rather effectively with women at the social level. The co-therapist then discontinued her participation in therapy.

With Kent's aversion to women significantly reduced, attention was then directed to the weakening of his sexual attraction to men. The first method used to aid in the achievement of this objective was aversive conditioning. The client would view provocative pictorial male stimuli and then be asked to imagine negative scenes such as being nauseated to the point of painful vomiting or becoming infected with ugly boils and sores over the entire body. This was continued until the pictures were repulsive rather than attractive to the client. The result was generalized fairly well to the client's real environment but short of the desired goal. While the client found males in general to have little or no stimulus effect, his homosexual friend yet remained a provocative stimulus. Two additional measures were employed to overcome this situation. Covert sensitization was first used to weaken the undesirable response habit. After training the client to relax, he would sit in a large comfortable armchair with his eyes closed and visualize his homosexual friend. When he indicated by a raised hand that he was highly stimulated by the image of the companion, he was asked to imagine his feeling sick at stomach, becoming more and more nauseated, and then vomiting all over himself, his friend, the furniture, and the room in which they were located. The client was also trained to be assertive in resisting the friend's moves toward sexual behavior. Kent decided eventually to end the relationship with the homosexual companion.

Two of the three final sessions were devoted to modeling and rehearsing assertive behaviors which the client wished to actualize in his work situation. The behaviors included the ability to present an idea and argue its merits, the ability to disagree constructively with a superior or senior colleague, and the ability to speak up when an injustice or unfair/unethical practice is evident.

In the final session, a review was made of the counseling-therapy process and the prospects for the future were discussed. The therapy covered an eight-months period of time, and the goals established for the process were successfully met. Neither of the methods used accounted singularly for the behavior change. Rather, it was the combination of the various modes of therapy that enabled the client to relate meaningfully and enjoyably to both males and females at the social level. Kent had gained a stronger desire for a heterosexual marriage, but he, as well as the counselor-therapist, realized that before he would be able to establish sexual intimacy with a woman he would probably need further therapy.

5

Epilogue

This volume is premised on the assumption that a bona fide system of integrative counseling and psychotherapy responsive to the myriad of human concerns reflects the need and emerging Zeitgeist of the hour. The thoughts presented herein were developed from the position that any single approach to psychotherapy neither possesses the theory and concepts necessary to comprehend the nature of man and human behavior, nor is equipped with therapeutic methods adequate to assist a cross-sectional clientele presenting the gamut of problems encountered in living. Rather, the psychotherapeutic truth lies in the intelligent and systematic integration of the best elements derived from all the schools of counseling and psychotherapy. This work has sought, and is intended, to serve as a respectable model for the integrative process from laying the foundation of a personalized theory of psychotherapy to implementing the theory in practice.

We accept unequivocally that differences in psychotherapy theory and practice have a heuristic effect and are desirable for this if for no other reason. Professional counseling and psychotherapy with its breadth and multiplicity could not have possibly evolved to the present status without the provocative influence of all the precursors. The vigorous search for a better understanding of human behavior and the discovery of more effective counseling-therapy technology must be ever encouraged. But if there is one thing that the helping professions and contemporary man need less of it is fragmentizing polarity. Spirited antagonism between and the tendency toward mutual exclusiveness of schools of psychotherapy do little to further the cause of mankind or to enhance the professional status of counseling and psychotherapy.

There is ground for the belief that the counseling profession would be strengthened by a pervasive spirit of reconciliatory integration. But such a spirit is possible *only* when psychotherapists are devoted more to the welfare of mankind than to their ideology. A religious proverb states that where an individual's treasure is there will his heart or devotion be also. Each counselor-therapist should ask himself, "What is the object of my devotion, maximal assistance to human beings with personality and behavior needs or the security of a theoretical system?" The answer to this question reveals that a) we have established our priorities, and b) either we are open to change and possessed of a willingness to adopt any available resource to help a client, or we are committed to an inflexible perpetuation of a personally endorsed system of exclusive theoretical dogma.

The logical place to initiate the process of integration is in counselor training programs. Counselor educators can do much to stimulate, encourage, and facilitate the integrative enterprise. (1) They can model philosophical and theoretical openness before their trainees. Rather than espousing a particular school of psychotherapy, counselor educators would do well to follow a "liberal arts" approach to the investigation of psychotherapeutic systems. (2) Trainers should provide counselor trainees with numerous modules of experiential learning in pre-practicum laboratories. The focus would be on the development of a core of facilitative human relationship skills and first-hand experimentation with a wide variety of therapeutic methods. (3) Counselor educators should require trainees to demonstrate empirically in the practicum that they are in command of both a core of interpersonal relationship skills and an armamentarium of counseling-therapy techniques that can be applied effectively to diverse client-problem situations. (4) Counselor educators should be involved in arranging integrative and interdisciplinary-oriented seminars and internships for trainees and encouraging their participation in these advanced learning opportunities.

Comprehensive and multidimensional counseling and psychotherapy, whether in the academic setting or in real world practice, is possible only when the principle of synergy is operative. The elements derived from many sources must be blended and must function smoothly and harmoniously under a superordinate system. We postulate that love, defined as unconditional commitment to the furtherance of the good of mankind that is manifested through purposeful and observable operations, possesses the greatest potential to serve as the synergistic agent to achieve transcendence of the polarity of conflicting therapy systems and to integrate the separate strengths into a functional whole.

BIBLIOGRAPHY

Adler, A. *The individual psychology of Alfred Adler.* H. L. & R. R. Ansbacher (Eds.). New York: Harper & Row, 1956.

——. *Problems of neurosis.* H. L. Ansbacher (Ed.). New York: Harper & Row, 1964.

——. *Superiority and social interest.* H. L. & R. R. Ansbacher (Eds.). New York: Viking, 1973.

Alexander, F. *Fundamentals of psychoanalysis.* New York: Norton, 1963.

Allport, G. W. *Becoming.* New Haven, Conn.: Yale University Press, 1955.

——. The open system in personality theory. *Journal of abnormal and social psychology,* 1961, *61,* pp. 301–310.

——. Psychological models for guidance. *Harvard educational review,* 1962, *32,* pp. 373–381.

——. The fruits of eclecticism: Bitter or sweet. *Acta psychologia,* 1964, *23,* pp. 27–44.

——. *The person in psychology.* Boston: Beacon, 1968.

Bandura, A. *Principles of behavior modification.* New York: Holt, Rinehart & Winston, 1969.

Beck, C. E. *Philosophical foundations of guidance.* Englewood Cliffs, N.J.: Prentice-Hall, 1963.

Berne, E. *Transactional analysis in psychotherapy.* New York: Grove Press, 1961.

——. *Group treatment.* New York: Grove Press, 1966.

——. *What do you say after you say hello?* New York: Grove Press, 1972.

Bernstein, D. A., & Borkovec, T. D. *Progressive relaxation training.* Champaign, Ill.: Research Press, 1973.

Billings, E. G. *A handbook of elementary psychobiology and psychiatry.* New York: Macmillan, 1939.

Blocher, D. H. *Developmental counseling.* New York: Ronald, 1966.

Bordin, E. S. *Psychological counseling* (2nd ed.). New York: Appleton-Century-Crofts, 1968.

Boring, E. G. The psychology of controversy. *The psychological review,* 1929, *36,* pp. 97–121.

Boss, M. *Psychoanalysis and Daseinanalysis.* New York: Basic Books, 1963.

Boy, A. V., & Pine, G. J. *The counselor in the schools.* Boston: Houghton Mifflin, 1968.

Brammer, L. M., & Shostrom, E. L. *Therapeutic psychology* (2nd ed.). Englewood Cliffs, N.J.: Prentice-Hall, 1968.

Brammer, L. M. Eclecticism revisited. *Personnel and guidance journal,* 1969, *48,* pp. 192–197.

————. *The helping relationship.* Englewood Cliffs, N.J.: Prentice-Hall, 1973.

Brussel, J. A., & Cantzlaar, G. L. *The layman's dictionary of psychiatry.* New York: Barnes & Noble, 1967.

Callis, R. Toward an integrated theory of counseling. *Journal of college student personnel,* 1960, *1,* pp. 2–9.

Carkhuff, R. R., & Berenson, B. G. *Beyond counseling and psychotherapy.* New York: Holt, Rinehart & Winston, 1967.

Cunningham, L. M., & Peters, H. J. *Counseling theories.* Columbus, Ohio: Charles E. Merrill, 1973.

Di Loreto, A. O. *Comparative psychotherapy.* Chicago: Aldine-Atherton, 1971.

Dollard, J., & Miller, N. E. *Personality and psychotherapy.* New York: McGraw-Hill, 1950.

Dustin, R., & George, R. *Action counseling for behavior change.* New York: Intext, 1973.

Ellis, A. *Humanistic psychotherapy: The rational-emotive approach.* New York: Julian, 1973a.

————. Rational-emotive therapy, in R. Corsini (Ed.), *Current psychotherapies.* Itasca, Ill.: Peacock, 1973b, pp. 167–206.

English, H. B., & English, A. C. *A comprehensive dictionary of psychological and psychoanalytical terms.* New York: David McKay, 1958.

Enright, J. B. An introduction to Gestalt techniques, in J. Fagan & I. L. Shepherd (Eds.), *Gestalt therapy now.* New York: Harper & Row, 1970, pp. 107–124.

Erikson, E. H. *Childhood and society.* New York: Norton, 1950.

————. *Identity and the life cycle.* New York: International Universities Press, 1959.

Farrelly, F., & Brandsma, J. *Provocative therapy.* Ft. Collins, Colo.: Shields, 1974.

Fine, R. Psychoanalysis, in R. Corsini (Ed.), *Current psychotherapies.* Itasca, Ill.: Peacock, 1973, pp. 1–33.

Ford, D. H., & Urban, H. B. *Systems of psychotherapy.* New York: John Wiley, 1963.

Frankl, V. E. *Man's search for meaning.* Boston: Beacon, 1962.

———. *The doctor and the soul* (2nd ed.). New York: Knopf, 1965.

———. *The will to meaning.* New York: New American Library, 1969.

Freud, S. *Beyond the pleasure principle.* New York: Liveright, 1970.

Fromm, E. *The sane society.* Greenwich, Conn.: Fawcett, 1955.

———. *The art of loving.* New York: Bantam Books, 1963.

Glasser, W. *Reality therapy.* New York: Harper & Row, 1965.

———. *The identity society.* New York: Harper & Row, 1972.

Glasser, W., & Zunin, L. M. Reality therapy, in R. Corsini (Ed.), *Current psychotherapies.* Itasca, Ill.: Peacock, 1973, pp. 287–315.

Harper, R. A. *Psychoanalysis and psychotherapy: 36 systems.* Englewood Cliffs, N.J.: Prentice-Hall, 1959.

Harris, T. A. *I'm OK — You're OK.* New York: Harper & Row, 1969.

Havighurst, R. J. *Developmental tasks and education.* (3rd ed.). New York: David McKay, 1972.

Hopke, W. E. *Dictionary of personnel and guidance terms.* Chicago: Ferguson, 1968.

Horney, K. *Our inner conflicts.* New York: Norton, 1945.

———. *Neurosis and human growth.* New York: Norton, 1953.

Jacobson, E. *Progressive relaxation.* Chicago: University of Chicago Press, 1938.

James, M., & Jongeward, D. *Born to win.* Reading, Mass.: Addison-Wesley, 1973.

James, W. *Pragmatism.* New York: Longmans, Green & Company, 1907.

Jung, C. G. *Analytical psychology.* New York: Random House, 1968.

Jurjevich, R. M. (Ed.) *Direct psychotherapy.* Coral Gables, Fla.: University of Miami Press, 1973, 2 vols.

Kanfer, F. H., & Saslow, G. Behavioral diagnosis, in C. M. Franks (Ed.), *Behavior Therapy.* New York: McGraw-Hill, 1969, pp. 417–444.

Kanfer, F. H., & Phillips, J. S. *Learning foundations of behavior therapy.* New York: John Wiley, 1970.

Kemp, C. G. *Intangibles in counseling.* Boston: Houghton Mifflin, 1967.

Kempler, W. Gestalt therapy, in R. Corsini (Ed.), *Current psychotherapies.* Itasca, Ill.: Peacock, 1973, pp. 251–286.

Krumboltz, J. D. Behavioral goals for counseling. *Journal of counseling psychology,* 1966, *13,* pp. 153–159.

Krumboltz, J. D., & Thoresen, C. E. (Eds.) *Behavioral counseling.* New York: Holt, Rinehart & Winston, 1969.

Landsman, T. Positive experience and the beautiful person. Presidential Address, Southeastern Psychological Association, April 1968, mimeographed.

Lazarus, A. A. In support of technical eclecticism. *Psychological reports,* 1967, *21,* pp. 415–416.

Levitsky, A., & Perls, F. S. The rules and games of Gestalt therapy, in J. Fagan & I. L. Shepherd (Eds.), *Gestalt therapy now.* New York: Harper & Row, 1970, pp. 140–149.

Lewin, K. *A dynamic theory of personality.* New York: McGraw-Hill, 1935.

Lief, A. (Ed.) *The common sense psychiatry of Adolf Meyer.* New York: McGraw-Hill, 1948.

London, P. *The modes and morals of psychotherapy.* New York: Holt, Rinehart & Winston, 1964.

Mahrer, A. R. The goals and families of psychotherapy: Summary, in A. R. Mahrer (Ed.), *The goals of psychotherapy.* New York: Appleton-Century-Crofts, 1967, pp. 259–269.

Marzolf, S. S. *Psychological diagnosis and counseling in the schools.* New York: Holt, Rinehart & Winston, 1956.

Maskin, A. Adaptations of psychoanalytic technique to specific disorders, in J. H. Masserman (Ed.), *Science and psychoanalysis.* Vol. 3. *Psychoanalysis and human values.* New York: Grune & Stratton, 1960, pp. 321–352.

Maslow, A. H. *Motivation and personality.* New York: Harper & Row, 1954.

———. *Eupsychian management.* Homewood, Ill.: Dorsey, 1965.

———. A theory of meta motivation: The biological rooting of the value life. *Journal of humanistic psychology,* 1967, 7, pp. 93–127.

———. Personality problems and personality growth. *College student journal,* 1971, 5, pp. 1–13.

May, R. *Love and will.* New York: Norton, 1969.

Montagu, A. A scientist looks at love. *Phi Delta Kappan,* 1970a, *51,* pp. 463–467.

———. *The direction of human development.* New York: Hawthorn Books, 1970b.

Mosak, H. H., & Shulman, B. H. The life style inventory. H. H. Mosak & B. H. Shulman, 1971.

Mosak, H. H., & Dreikurs, R. Adlerian psychotherapy, in R. Corsini (Ed.), *Current psychotherapies.* Itasca, Ill.: Peacock, 1973, pp. 35–83.

Munroe, R. L. *Schools of psychoanalytic thought.* New York: Holt, Rinehart & Winston, 1955.

O'Neill, N., & O'Neill, G. *Open marriage.* New York: Evans, 1972.

Osipow, S. H., & Walsh, W. B. *Strategies in counseling for behavior change.* New York: Appleton-Century-Crofts, 1970.

Patterson, C. H. *Counseling and psychotherapy.* New York: Harper & Row, 1959.

———. *Theories of counseling and psychotherapy* (2nd ed.). New York: Harper & Row, 1973.

Perls, F., Hefferline, R. F., & Goodman, P. *Gestalt therapy.* New York: Dell, 1951.

Perls, F. *Gestalt therapy verbatim.* Moab, Utah: Real People Press, 1969.

Prescott, D.A. Role of love in human development. *Journal of home economics,* 1952, *44,* pp. 173–176.

Ritter, B. Eliminating excessive fears of the environment through contact desensitization, in J. D. Krumboltz & C. E. Thoresen (Eds.), *Behavioral Counseling.* New York: Holt, Rinehart & Winston, 1969, pp. 168–178.

Rogers, C. R. The necessary and sufficient conditions of therapeutic personality change. *Journal of consulting psychology,* 1957, *21,* pp. 95–103.

––––––. A theory of therapy, personality, and interpersonal relationships, as developed in the client-centered framework, in S. Koch (Ed.), *Psychology: A study of science,* Vol. III. *Formulations of the person and the social context.* New York: McGraw-Hill, 1959, pp. 184–256.

––––––. *On becoming a person.* Boston: Houghton Mifflin, 1961.

Rogers, C. R., & Dymond, R. F. *Psychotherapy and personality change.* Chicago: University of Chicago Press, 1954.

Rychlak, J. F. *Introduction to personality and psychotherapy.* Boston: Houghton Mifflin, 1973.

Sahakian, W. S. Psychobiologic therapy, in W. S. Sahakian (Ed.), *Psychotherapy and counseling.* Chicago: Rand McNally, 1969, pp. 373–392.

Shostrom, E. L. Love, the human encounter, in H. A. Otto (Ed.), *Love today.* New York: Association Press, 1972, pp. 185–196.

Skinner, B. F. *Science and human behavior.* New York: Macmillan, 1953.

––––––. *Beyond freedom and dignity.* New York: Knopf, 1971.

Slavson, S. R. Eclecticism versus sectarianism in group psychotherapy. *International journal of group psychotherapy,* 1970, *20,* pp. 3–13.

Smith, D. Love: The synergistic agent in the helping process. Unpublished paper, 1973.

Sorokin, P. A. *The ways and power of love.* Chicago: Henry Regnery, 1967.

Stein, M. J. (Ed.) *Contemporary psychotherapies.* New York: Free Press, 1961.

Sullivan, H. S. *The interpersonal theory of psychiatry.* H. S. Perry & M. L. Gawel (Eds.) New York: Norton, 1953.

Szasz, T. S. The myth of mental illness. *American psychologist,* 1960, *15,* pp. 113–118.

––––––. *The myth of mental illness.* New York: Dell, 1961.

––––––. The myth of mental illness: Three addenda. *Journal of humanistic psychology,* 1974, *14,* pp. 11–19.

Thompson, C. *Psychoanalysis: Evolution and development.* New York: Grove Press, 1950.

Thorne, F. C. *Principles of psychological examining.* Brandon, Vt.: Journal of Clinical Psychology, 1955.

––––––. *Personality.* Brandon, Vt.: Journal of Clinical Psychology, 1961a.

––––––. *Clinical judgment.* Brandon, Vt.: Journal of Clinical Psychology, 1961b.

————. *Tutorial counseling.* Brandon, Vt.: Journal of Clinical Psychology, 1965.

————. *Integrative psychology.* Brandon, Vt.: Journal of Clinical Psychology, 1967.

———— *Psychological case handling.* Brandon, Vt.: Journal of Clinical Psychology, 1968.

————. An eclectic evaluation of psychotherapeutic methods, in R. M. Jurjevich (Ed.), *Direct psychotherapy.* Vol. 2. Coral Gables, Fla.: University of Miami Press, 1973a, pp. 847–883.

————. Eclectic psychotherapy, in R. Corsini (Ed.), *Current psychotherapies.* Itasca, Ill.: Peacock, 1973b, pp. 445–486.

Truax, C. B., & Carkhuff, R. R. *Toward effective counseling and psychotherapy.* Chicago: Aldine-Atherton, 1967.

Truax, C. B., & Mitchell, K. M. Research on certain therapist interpersonal skills in relation to process and outcome, in A. E. Bergin & S. L. Garfield (Eds.), *Handbook of psychotherapy and behavior change.* New York: John Wiley, 1971, pp. 299–344.

Tweedie, D. F. *Logotherapy.* Grand Rapids, Mich.: Baker, 1961.

Ullmann, L. P., & Krasner, L. *A psychological approach to abnormal behavior.* Englewood Cliffs, N.J.: Prentice-Hall, 1969.

van Kaam, A. Existential psychology as a comprehensive theory of personality. *Existential psychology and psychiatry,* 1963, *3,* pp. 11–26.

————. *Existential foundations of psychology.* Pittsburgh, Pa.: Duquesne University Press, 1966.

Wallen, R. Gestalt therapy and Gestalt psychology, in J. Fagan & J. L. Shepherd (Eds.), *Gestalt therapy now.* New York: Harper & Row, 1971, pp. 8–13.

White, R. W. The concept of healthy personality: What do we really mean? *The counseling psychologist,* 1973, *4* (2), pp. 3–12.

Wildman, R. W., & Wildman, R. W., Jr. The practice of clinical psychology in the United States. *Journal of clinical psychology,* 1967, *23,* pp. 292–295.

Williamson, E. G. *Vocational counseling.* New York: McGraw-Hill, 1965.

Wolberg, L. R. *The technique of psychotherapy.* New York: Grune & Stratton, 1954.

Wolpe, J. *The practice of behavior therapy* (2nd ed.). New York: Pergamon, 1973.

Wolpe, J., & Lazarus, A. A. *Behavior therapy techniques.* New York: Pergamon, 1966.

Woodworth, R. S. *Contemporary schools of psychology* (3rd ed.). New York: Ronald, 1964. (1st ed. 1931; revised ed. 1948.)

Woody, R. H. *Psychobehavioral counseling and therapy.* New York: Appleton-Century-Crofts, 1971.

INDEX

Abnormality, 37, 52
Abraham, K., 3
Action Counseling, 11
Active Analytical Psychotherapy, 3
Active imagination, 86
Adler, A., 3, 11, 72
Adolescence, 48
Adulthood, 49, 50
Agape (See Love)
Alexander, F., 3, 87
Allport, G. W., 8, 13, 15, 30, 31, 37, 42
Analytical Psychology, 3
Assertive training, 74, 104
Aversion therapy, 78, 79, 112
Aversive imagery, 78
Bandura, A., 4, 77
Beck, C. E., 31
Behavior modification, 11, 17, 19, 25, 36
Behavior Therapy, 4, 73–79
Behavioral analysis (See Counseling-
    therapy)
Behavioral rehearsal or role playing, 74
Berenson, B. G., 14
Berne, E., 4, 38
Bernstein, D. A., 75
Bibliotherapy, 77, 88, 89
Blocher, D. H., 9
Body, 34, 37
Bordin, E. S., 10, 11
Boring, E. G., 4, 15, 26
Borkovec, T. D., 75
Boss, M., 63
Brammer, L. M., 10, 13, 14, 15, 17, 60, 89
Brandsma, J., 4
Breuer, J., 2
Brussel, J. A., 36
Callis, R., 14
Cantzlaar, G. L., 36
Carkhuff, R. R., 14, 64
Character Analysis, 3
Charcot, J., 2
Childhood, 47, 48
Client-Centered Therapy, 4, 79, 87

Conditioned Reflex Therapy, 4
Conscience, 38
Contact desensitization, 77, 78
Counseling and psychotherapy
    the and/or question, 18
    denominational, 4ff.
    divergent theories, 2ff.
    forms of, 55–57
    motives for, 55
    the nature of, 54
    systems of, 3, 4
Counseling-therapy, the process of be-
        havioral analysis or diagnosis,
        65–69, 100–102, 105–109
    relationship
        demonstrating love, 63–65
        handling resistance, 60
        initial contact, 59, 60
        orientation, 61, 62
        structure, 62
        transference-counter transfer-
            ence 62, 63
    statement of goals, 69, 70, 102, 103,
        109
    termination, 95–98
    therapeutic methods and strategies,
        70–95
Covert sensitization, 78, 112
Cunningham, L. M., 4
Darwin, C., 30
Daseinanalyse, 3
De-reflection, 80, 81, 104
Developmental Counseling, 9
Developmental history, 67, 101, 107
Didactic therapy, 87, 88
Di Loreto, A. O., 5
Directed awareness, 84, 85
Dollard, J., 9, 62
Dreamwork, 85
Dreikurs, R., 71
Dualism, 27
Dustin, R., 11, 12
Dynamic Psychotherapy, 3

Man, the nature of
 in the imagine of God view, 31–32
 mechanical view, 30
 a personal view of, 34–35
 phylogenetic view, 30, 31
 rational animal or classical view, 31
 role in counseling and
  psychotherapy theory and
  practice, 29, 30
Marzolf, S. S., 13
Maskin, A., 6
Maslow, A. H., 29, 37, 41, 42, 43
May, R., 39, 64
Mental illness (See Abnormality)
Meyer, A., 3, 8
Miller, N. E., 9, 62
Mind, 34, 38, 39
Modeling, 77, 112
Montagu, A. A., 41, 64
Mosak, H. H., 71, 72
Motivation (See Personality, dynamics
 of)
Mysticism, 3
Needs (See Personality, dynamics of)
Neurosis, 1, 2, 3
Nous (See Mind)
O'Neill, N. and G., 28
Operant conditioning, 73, 77
Orgone therapy, 3
Osipow, S. H., 11, 66
Paradoxical intention, 80
Particularism, 27, 28
Pattern construct, 26
Patterson, C. H., 15
Perls, F. S., 4, 37, 39, 81, 83, 85
Person (See also Personality)
 as an actualizing unique individual,
  36, 37
 the decisive, 39
 as an experiencing organism in a
  phenomenal universe, 44, 45
 the feeling, 38
 illustrated diagramatically, 44, 46
 motivated by needs, 40–43
 the physical, 37
 the self-conscious, 39
 the spiritual, 39
 the thinking, 38
 the valuing, 38
Personality
 definition, 36, 37
 development of, 43–51
 disordered or problematic, causes of
  existential crises, 54
  inappropriate learning, 53
  unmet basic needs, 53
 dynamics of, 40–43
 healthy, 37, 51, 52

structure of, 37–40
Peters, H. J., 4
Phenomenal field, 44, 45, 46
Phenomenal universe, 44, 52
Philia (See Love)
Phillips, J. S., 66
Pneuma (See Spirit)
Positional analysis, 93, 95
Positive reinforcement, 73, 74
Pragmatism, 7
Prescott, D. A., 64
Progressivism, 9
Provocative Therapy, 4
Psyche, 34, 38, 39
Psychoanalysis, 2, 3, 9, 86
Psychobiologic Therapy, 3, 8, 9, 11
Psychotherapy (See Counseling and
 psychotherapy)
Rank, O., 3, 11
Rational-Emotive Psychotherapy, 4, 56,
 87
Reality Therapy, 4, 38, 56, 88
Reductionism, 26, 27, 28
Reflection, 79
Reich, W., 3
Relaxation Therapy, 3
Resistance, 60
Ritter, B., 78
Rogers, C. R., 4, 30, 35, 37, 38, 41, 52, 58,
 59, 79
Role-playing, 74
Rychlak, J. F., 26, 37, 55
Salter, A., 4
Saslow, G., 66
Script analysis, 93, 95
Self-actualizing, 34, 37, 39, 42, 43, 49,
 52, 53, 54
Self, self-concept, 40, 45
Shostrom, E. L., 10, 13, 14, 64, 89
Shulman, B. H., 72
Shutz, 4
Skinner, B. F., 27, 73
Slavson, S. R., 14
Social-Psychological Analysis, 3
Soma (See Body)
Sorokin, P. A., 64
Soul (See *Psyche*)
Spirit, 34, 39
Stein, M. J., 6
Stekel, W., 3
Storge (See Love)
Structural analysis, 91, 92
Substance construct, 26
Sullivan, H. S., 3
Superego, 38
Synergy
 definition, 28, 29
 equated with love, 29